The Superstitions of THE IRRELIGIOUS

The Superstitions

OF

THE

IRRELIGIOUS

by GEORGE HEDLEY

GREENWOOD PRESS, PUBLISHERS
WESTPORT, CONNECTICUT

Library of Congress Cataloging in Publication Data

Hedley, George Percy, 1899-
    The superstitions of the irreligious.

    Reprint of the ed. published by Macmillan, New York.
    1. Irreligion--Controversial literature. I. Title.
[BL2747.H43 1979]   239   78-10274
ISBN 0-313-20755-0

BL2747
H43
1979

Reprinted with the permission of Macmillan Publishing Co., Inc.

Reprinted in 1979 by Greenwood Press, Inc.
51 Riverside Avenue, Westport, CT 06880

Printed in the United States of America

10 9 8 7 6 5 4 3 2 1

'Ye men of Athens, I perceive that in all things ye are too superstitious.'—Acts 17:22, 'King James' version, 1611.

'Men of Athens, I perceive that in every way you are very religious.'—Acts 17:22, Revised Standard Version, 1946.

PREFACE

My thanks are due first to the two Lynn Townsend Whites, who jointly started me on this enterprise: Dr. White the father, Professor Emeritus in San Francisco Theological Seminary, and Dr. White the son, President of Mills College. They chanced to hear together a Chapel sermon under this title, and together they agreed that more was to be said in detail.

I am grateful also to the editors of two 'magazines of national circulation,' to whom I sent a 2500-word script which was substantially that of the sermon, for two of the most gracious rejection notes I ever have received. They too said that the argument needed expansion by way of specification; and so they too have a share in my decision to expand and specify.

My honored colleague Darius Milhaud was so kind as to read the pages dealing with music, and so generous as to pass them for substance of doctrine. To others of our Mills faculty as well I owe untellable gratitude for continuing intellectual stimulus, largely conveyed over the coffee cups at 10:00 MWF. I shall not try to list them: their names fill twelve pages in the current College catalogue, and may be looked up there.

A woman colleague remarked recently, 'The trouble with a woman professor is that she doesn't have a wife to look after her.' This was with direct reference to my well-known dependence on Helen Campbell Hedley, who listens with patience and comments in sanity and shrewdness whenever I come charging from the study with a first draft. I owe her all that matters most; and more of the same for her help on this job.

The only part of the material which has been published previously consists in a few paragraphs which I have lifted from a 1947 assembly speech at the University of Oregon, which appeared in *Vital Speeches* that autumn. I acknowledge with thanks the permission to reproduce which the editors of that journal have granted.

Since this is a book for reading rather than for reference, I have omitted the conventional end matter of bibliography, notes, and index. The Biblical quotations may be identified quickly by thumbing through a Concordance. They are from the 'King James' version except in one Psalm verse for which I have used the Great Bible's phrasing, and one freehand rendering of my own from St. Paul. For other materials quoted I have tried to give due credit, and sufficient reference, in the text. So far as I know, I have borrowed nothing which stands under copyright.

My final thanks go to my 'irreligious' friends about whom the book is written, and to whom primarily it is addressed. I thank them for their friendship most of all; but also for their frankness of utterance, for their continual challenge to one's thinking, for their gay good temper in the midst of the most heated disputes. The situation seems to be that we respect each other's minds, except on this one point of religion.

If they will read what follows, I shall have a higher regard for their intellectual curiosity. If they should at all be influenced by it, I shall of course have more enthusiasm for their judgment. But in any event I shall continue sincerely and happily to like them.

G. H.

Ruddigore
Mills College
Maundy Thursday 1951

CONTENTS

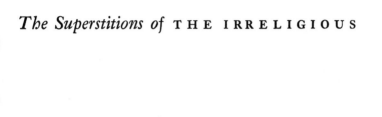

The Superstitions of T H E I R R E L I G I O U S

INTRODUCTION

on the nature and
prevalence of superstition

⏼ Anyone who is at all a member of a modern metropolitan community, and especially anyone who lives and works on a College campus, will know at once what this book is about. The irreligious make up a large proportion of the American population of today; and the consciously and vocally irreligious make up a sizable proportion of that proportion. For the present purpose I am not primarily concerned with those who, having given up religion, are mildly apologetic about the fact. They no doubt need evangelization; or propaganda, if you will. But the word for them is other than that which herein I shall be trying to say.

Rather I am thinking of, and (no doubt by indirection) addressing myself to, those who have given up religion and who think to be proud of their surrender. These are in part the hardheaded business men who conceive that the Golden Rule simply won't work in the economic world, and who are honest enough therefore to stay away from those places where the Golden Rule most commonly is proclaimed. In part (and only marginally in contrast) they are the explicit followers of Karl Marx, who accept the dictum about 'the opium of the people' as part of the truth once for all committed to the scientific socialists. Most of all they are the self-conscious intellectuals who are quite sure that religion is outmoded, that it is wholly beneath the notice of men and women of emancipated mind.

These last I know particularly well, and with many of them I share a warm and genuine friendship. That friendship endures despite the fact that for years I have found myself getting more and more fed up with these people. I am fed up: to say the worst at the outset: I am fed up with them because they know so pathetically little in the field of religion; because they know so much in that field that simply isn't so; because they exhibit themselves as totally unwilling to learn; and because, with all these things true, they still insist on talking. Much the same is true of the Marxist irreligious; and only at the point of lesser loquacity on the subject are the business men noticeably different. Thus my concern is partly with Wall Street and its San Francisco counterpart of Montgomery Street, or with Main Street in Zenith. But my principal unhappiness is rather about Greenwich Village on the Atlantic and Telegraph Hill on the Pacific, and about those on every campus who are so eager 'to hear or tell some new thing' that they cannot see the things which are old and enduring.

I am calling these people 'irreligious' because they have chosen to call themselves so. 'Unchurched' probably would be a more accurate description, but to them it would seem a hopelessly stuffy one. The extent of their real irreligiousness depends on how one chooses to define 'religion'; and since that choice marks the crux of my quarrel with them, the measurement involves the whole subject before us.

While in their chosen definition of religion they will readily accept my calling them 'irreligious,' they will resent immediately my using of the word 'superstitious.' Yet that word belongs here: for they have superstition, and it has them. 'Superstition' is a matter of something standing over one, something unexamined and awe-inspiring. Thus it is for the superstitious person a matter of his standing under something he does not understand, something that therefore he is afraid of. What these people stand under is a texture of misunderstandings. 'Stand' is an exact word, too. Very positively they don't 'labor under' their misapprehensions about religion. If they did, they would stand more chance of getting out.

The hallmark of superstition is unwillingness to examine the facts in a given case. The victim of superstition lives under compulsions which he not only does not understand, but which also he refuses to try to understand. The irreligious sophisticate is very sure (and at times of course he is right in this sureness) that religion has been marked historically by just such an unwillingness to test assumption by evidence, to examine means before assigning causes, to check subjective feelings by reference to objective facts. *Ergo,* says the anti-religionist, religious people are controlled by superstition.

Yet just the same phenomena appear on this other side of the fence. Was the mediaeval Christian layman illiterate in theology? The modern anti-Christian surely is no more learned here. Is the devout pietist dominated by memories of his childhood instruction and his childish fears? The proudly impious yet persist in judging all religion by their own childhood memories of those particular modes of religious expression to which they happened to be exposed. Is the simple believer unready to listen to, or to learn, anything that runs counter to attitudes which uncritically he has adopted once and for ever? Before the complicated unbelievers begin to throw stones, they had better barricade their own glass houses of preconception and prejudgment.

Thus the whole issue is just that of superstition *versus* sober enquiry, whether within the religious tradition or outside it. The plea I would make is that those who think to damn religion shall pause first to learn something about it. If they are devotees of science, they are required to examine all the evidence: not only the bits of evidence that seem to support their own present views. If they are 'socially conscious' members of human society, they are obligated to study that society in terms of its real history, its real structure, its real motivations, rather than to retreat into the intellectual abstractions (or, rather, the intellectual creations *ex nihilo*) which demand so much less actual thinking and so very much less hard work. If they would be spokesmen of the new generation, if they would be members of the world that ought to be, they must acquaint themselves with the world that is and has been, with what all the former generations have learned and with what they have chosen to forget.

Until the declared foemen of religion meet these requirements, they stand condemned as being superstitious indeed. The pages that follow use as outline some of the assumptions and clichés that characterize current non-religious and anti-religious talking. They seek, however, to ask some of the questions which as yet most of the irreligious have declined even to hear, let alone to answer. The hope of finding a common answer depends upon the capacity of all of us, on both sides, to free ourselves from superstition as we study the relevant data.

SUPERSTITION NO. 1

*that the content and emphasis of religious
thought and teaching undergo no change*

◖◗ Our friends should know better than to maintain this first of their superstitions, that of the immutability of the religious species, especially in view of their insistence that religion is a purely human invention. The more human, the more responsive to pressures; and the pressures upon religion are and have been continuous, though themselves ever changing. Thus the first demand that must be made upon all who discuss religion, whether eventually to accept or to repudiate, is that they shall qualify themselves as students of religion's history.

It is to be admitted that many now middle-aged Americans got off to a peculiarly unhappy start in their earliest religious contacts. They were youngsters in the last and worst days of gingerbread decoration, and they learned long ago to sneer at the furniture and the architecture of their youth. Brought up in a culture that was basically agrarian, with many frontier overtones, they have grown up as, and into, civilized urbanites. The Church they first knew was physically gingerbread, the Sunday School temperamentally rural; and these they have thrown overboard with the other discards from their childhood.

One assumption of our grandparents was that since religion was good for all people, the same kind of religious expression must be good for people of all ages. Accordingly they took their children to long preaching services which they couldn't possibly understand; and worse still, they insisted that the children should profess to religious experiences (called 'conviction of sin,' or 'repentance,' or 'redemption') which as children they couldn't possibly share. The spiritual food provided may or may not have been wholly good; but whether it was good or not, it wasn't a formula for babies.

Perhaps it is well that our modern protesters against this usage did not meet Albert Einstein until they got into Upper Division courses, John Dewey till they entered Teachers' College; or, on as good grounds as they can show for religion, they might have declared physics and philosophy unworthy of their notice. The odd thing about them is that, hyperconscious as they are of their own adulthood, they persist in measuring religion entirely by their infantile impressions of it. It won't wash: for not only have they changed during the years, but normative American religion has changed no less.

But the American part of the story is a late and minor one; and to understand it aright we shall have to go back much further into the past from which all our religious phenomena are derived. Does religion change? At least we have to say that historically religion has changed a great deal, and at many and varied points. Some years ago a clergyman, one whom my unbelieving friends and I would agree in calling 'superstitious,' argued in my hearing that the divine character of the Bible was proved by the fact (as he alleged it) that all the Biblical writers, living over a span of more than twelve hundred years, believed exactly the same doctrines and taught exactly the same ethics. Any competent scholar of today knows, even if the deprecators of religion do not, that nothing of the sort is true.

Quite to the contrary, the whole evidence of the Bible is to the effect that men's views of truth, their views of God, their views of the good life, were changing from generation to generation; and most careful readers will agree that the changes more commonly than not marked genuine growth. From a manlike being who went 'walking in the garden' of Eden 'in the cool of the day,' or who dropped in to visit Abraham in his encampment on the Judean highlands, God became the high and holy one who inhabits eternity, and the very hem of whose robe, in Isaiah's vision, filled the temple men had built to house him. From a jealous Oriental prince whom Joshua dissuaded from destroying Israel only by asking who then would be left to worship him, God became a loving Father who wiped away the people's iniquity and forgave their sins. From a tyrant who insisted upon formal and costly sacrifices, God became a friend whose requirement of man was but that he should deal justly, and love kindness, and walk humbly in the divine presence.

One striking illustration of such moral growth in the Old Testament period is provided in the treatment of human sacrifice. The early cycle of stories that took its form near Jerusalem, in about the ninth century B.C., tells us of Jephthah, who because of an ill-advised vow was impelled to sacrifice his beloved daughter in tribute to his God for a victory won. The narrator does seem to think that Jephthah swore hastily and thoughtlessly; but he betrays no notion that, once the vow was made, its maker could please God in any way save by carrying it out to its tragic termination. A hundred years afterward, in one of the Northern Israelite tales of the early days, Abraham is shown as learning that he does not have to sacrifice his son Isaac, despite a vow that he would; and without explicit statement of theory, the teller of this prophetic tale clearly implies that no human sacrifice ever is required by the God in whom he believes. A century later still, in the law book of Deuteronomy which seems to have been carefully hidden in the temple in order that it might be found there, human sacrifice at last is flatly condemned as being one of the worst abominations of the Canaanites.

Had religion changed? Certainly man's understanding of it had. The psychologist will note, however, that those who sought to present a new view were fully aware of conservative attitudes among their readers. Therefore both the Elohist who told of Abraham, and the Deuteronomist who was setting forth a revised code of moral law, referred their own judgments to a distant and respected past; and each of them thus embedded the change he was making in a tradition whose continuity he regarded as important.

When we turn from the Old Testament to the New, we find that Christianity also grew out of the soil of continuity into an atmosphere of decisive alteration. 'Think not,' the scribal editor of St. Matthew's Gospel quotes Jesus as saying, 'that I am come to destroy the law, or the prophets: I am not come to destroy, but to fulfil.' Yet no less than five successive times, further on in the same chapter, we find Jesus declaring, 'It was said to them of old time . . . but I say unto you . . .' In each of these cases the change is one from old rigidity to new freedom, from external rule to inner motive, from the letter to the spirit. The record indicates that Jesus came to be distrusted by the Jewish authorities precisely because he seemed to be promoting religious change, and that he was put to death by the Romans because he was regarded as a danger to the existing Roman world order.

Calling next the roll of heroes of the Christian faith in later times, we find that they were changers and upsetters and innovators too. 'These that have turned the world upside down,' protested the conservative and contented citizens of Thessalonica, 'are come hither also.' The Bishops of Rome sought to shift the center of world control from state to Church, because they held that particular change in government to be necessary to the doing of God's will upon the earth. St. Francis began his career as a rebel against official sterility in religion, and rendered his persisting service as the founder of a new Order. Martin Luther carried spiritual discontent on into ecclesiastical and then political revolt. John Calvin of the Presbyterians, and George Fox of the Quakers, and Roger Williams of the Baptists, and John Wesley of the Methodists, all were assailed as religious radicals; and appropriately so, for all of them assailed religion in that state in which they found it. The history of religious leadership is in its very essence the history of religious change and growth; and they who deny the occurrence of such evolutionary mutations in religion rank themselves with those wilfully blind creationists who thought once to stare Darwin out of countenance.

It happens that the North American story, as we know it, begins at one of the major periods of religious change in Western Europe. The seaboard colonies began to be settled just when the Protestant revolt against Rome was at its height, and the movement into the continental interior coincided with the rise of those radically Protestant sects which repudiated even the middle way of the Church of England. Once the geographical moves had been made, the contacts available with the old home in Europe were meagre. Accordingly the American Protestant pattern tended to crystallize just at the point of greatest opposition to Rome, and of the most violent rebellion against all former usages and judgments.

The striking illustrations of this mood were acute Biblicism on the one hand, and vigorous anti-ritualism on the other. They who had rejected the authority of the Church were scarcely ready to make the leap directly to the authority of the individual conscience; and so in place of the formal standard which they had repudiated, they set up another standard quite as formal and considerably less flexible. They maintained that the Bible was factually correct and morally unquestionable 'from cover to cover'; and they took it for granted that the Bible said precisely what, in their varied but often unscholarly judgments, they chose to understand it to say.

In taking this position the extreme Biblicists were ignoring not only Jesus' strictures upon certain elements in the laws of Moses, and St. Paul's insistence upon a 'new covenant, not of letter, but of spirit,' but also the actual Biblical views of the chief thinkers and leaders of the Protestant fellowships. Martin Luther not only had condemned the Epistle of St. James as *recht ströherne*, 'right strawy,' because it seemed to him to teach salvation by works rather than by faith. He also had commented that the book of Esther contained 'a superfluity of heathen naughtiness,' and he had set the book of Revelation in the appendix to his German Bible, along with the Apocrypha, in the obvious hope that his people would not pay too much attention to it. Wesley too, in revising the English *Book of Common Prayer* for use by the Methodist societies in America, had remarked that 'certain of the Psalms are not fit to be in a Christian's mouth.'

A special case of applied Biblicism appears in what came to be the prevailing Protestant mode of observance of Sunday. It was understood that this rested upon the regulations for the Sabbath which were set forth in the Jewish law; and one suspects that no little of modern distaste for religion can be traced to those dull and depressing Sundays in which little boys and girls found themselves imprisoned. It was accordingly a special delight to one such youngster, reading in his young manhood the *Institutes* of John Calvin, to discover that this hero of the dour Presbyterians had held that the Christian Sunday stood in no sort of organic connection with the Jewish Sabbath, and that its character should be one of active worship rather than of negative regulation. Only in the first years of the seventeenth century, through the contentions of a Puritan divine curiously but fittingly named Nicholas Bownd, did the Sabbath of Judaism get carried over into the special day of Christian religious observance; and only for a matter of some three hundred years, in a rather narrowly limited segment of Christendom, did the Reverend Mr. Bownd's judgment dominate the practice of professedly religious people.

In the days of the present writer's youth, some thirty years ago, the view that religion had changed in history, and that it should change yet more, commonly was called 'Modernism.' Protestant opposition to change from nineteenth-century religious patterns was described in general as 'Fundamentalism,' a term that is used less now than it was then. It is important to notice that 'Fundamentalism' as a technical word was invented only in America in the early twentieth century, with the publication of *The Fundamentals* in 1910 and the formation of 'The Christian Fundamentals League' in 1920. In point of historic fact, the views that the 'Fundamentalists' held, based all of them upon an absolutely literal acceptance of the Bible as authority in every field, never had characterized historic Christianity until some of the lesser followers of Martin Luther transmuted his soaring faith in the Bible's truth into a mechanical devotion to the Bible's words.

So-called 'Modernism,' on the other hand, while in its Protestant form undeniably superficial and flimsy in many of its expressions, was much more ancient and authentic in its Christian rootage. The type of criticism it tried to make of things as they were, was closely akin to the very criticisms that had been made by the Hebrew prophets, and by Jesus, and by all the major heroes of the faith in after years. Even in its specifically Biblical views 'Modernism' had notable precursors not only in Jesus and St. Paul on the one hand, and in such reformers as Luther and Calvin and Wesley on the other, but also in such Fathers of the Church as Chrysostom, who denied the divine authorization of the Temple ritual; and Theodore of Mopsuestia, who held many of the Psalms to be not Davidic, but rather post-exilic, and who denied the scriptural status of the general epistles and the book of Revelation; and Theodore's contemporary Cassiodorus, who argued that such documents as Psalm 22 were not predictive, but simply historical.

The long dominant anti-ritualism of American Protestant Christianity will come before us for special attention when we think of the nature and use of religious symbols. At this point it is enough to notice its effect in making worship sparse and often ugly, and in denying to adherents of the Protestant groups that treasury of beauty in sight and sound which the Church had created through the centuries. The architectural abominations of the Akron plan, the corresponding horrors of the Prince Albert coat as the uniform of the nonconformist clergy, and the banal intervals of the tunes of 'gospel songs,' all represent this temporary but powerful fear of the beautiful and the vitally symbolic in religious practice. Such horrors the irreligious of today are completely sound in rejecting, with any amount of horror in their faces and in their tones of voice. Their unsoundness lies in their supposing that religion, which for a brief time in a small area has suffered this sea-change of ugliness, is incapable of changing again toward beauty: toward beauty both long existent and yet to be created.

The summary of the historical case is that religion always has shown the capacity for change: mostly, it would seem, for the better, though now and then clearly for the worse. On the positive side religion has changed its emphases and its expressions with the great spirits of history, with the brave souls who dared to think for themselves and to say openly what they thought. Negatively, religion has suffered change of a far less happy sort when narrow minds have sought to constrict truth into their own narrow channels; and then matters have been made still worse when natural human conservatism has tried to conserve not true and abiding values, but certain limited forms that took their shape under particular social pressures and because of circumstantially determined intellectual judgments.

At this point the more literate members of the opposition to religion will raise a protest on the matter of definition. Quite accurately they will point out that the Latin *religio* is to be traced either to the verb *relegere*, 'to read over,' or to *religare*, 'to bind back.' In either case the effect would be the same. Religion would seem to involve the reading over of ancient documents, and also the binding back of one's thought and action to the practices and attitudes of former days. And if it is argued further that many religious people have been characterized by such a frame of mind, no reasonable and informed person will presume to deny the charge.

Yet herein it has been contended that religion has changed, and will change, and should change. Is there any resolution possible? There is, if we but succeed in making the one basic distinction between ultimate values and immediate manifestations. Religion ever exhibits itself in two primary aspects, in two poles between which all religious thought and expression must operate.

On the one hand we have man: ourselves, limited and fumbling and confused, here today and gone tomorrow. On the other hand we have truth: truth which is timeless, truth which is abiding, truth which never is to be destroyed. Religion, rightly understood, is none other than our effort to bring our limited selves into touch with the limitless truth of life, and so indeed to bind ourselves to the sources of all value.

Those who will not read religious literature, but who follow the publications of science with a degree of care, will remember that in the year 1935 Dr. Wendell Stanley made a crucial determination in the study of viruses: namely, that certain viruses appear in crystalline form, and thus that no sharp demarcation between organic and inorganic, between living and non-living beings, longer could be maintained. Does this mean that viruses never formed crystals before the year of grace 1935? Scarcely. Does it mean that until 1935 there was a firm barrier between the living and the non-living creations, a barrier which then Dr. Stanley wiped out? Not at all. All it means is that in 1935, by the agency of Professor Stanley and the electronic microscope, man for the first time saw crystals of types that had existed from the earliest aeons of the evolutionary process. What it means is that the natural world always has been a united whole, differentiated within itself not by absolute chasms but by an infinite series of almost imperceptible gradations: a fact of life and a truth of science that man at last had managed to learn. What had Dr. Stanley changed? Not the natural world, but our knowledge of it.

Does religion change? In the realm of the truth that it seeks, never. In the realm of our grasp of the truth, all of the time. The things that are seen are temporary. The things that are unseen, and they alone, are eternal. It was not God who changed, between the Jahvistic legends in the ninth century B.C. and the writing of the latter part of the book of Hosea two or three hundred years later, from a whimsical tyrant to a loving friend. It was man who had grown enough to realize that God must be greater and more gracious than was man himself. It was not essential ethical value that changed when Jesus began to teach.

It was Jesus who saw more clearly through fringe to center, through form to meaning, and who thereby changed man's ways of estimating what mattered most.

The objective of religion ever has been the same, and ever is the same: to know the truth and to live by it. The expression of religion, exactly for that reason, has to change continually, as day by day we learn a little more and are qualified to live a little better. They therefore who oppose all religious change are wilfully obscurantist; and they who deny that change has occurred are stubbornly ignorant.

Alike for religionists and for irreligionists there is needed a word of caution here as to the limited human realm itself. True learning, however new, always is built upon what men have learned before; and wise living never is to be achieved without taking account of life as men have lived it. Dr. Stanley's discoveries in biological science would be literally unthinkable but for the patient work of the generations of biologists and bacteriologists who have gone before; and Isaiah's vision of God, and Jesus' vision, and our own, have required the preparation of centuries of Israelite history, and centuries of Jewish faith, and centuries of Christian growth. Jesus, who challenged the old law at many points, came not to destroy it. He came rather to fulfill it, to fill it with meanings that men had not realized before.

To throw overboard all that mankind has learned and done in the former days is thoughtlessly to hurl ourselves backward into barbarism. A notable case in point is that of the countless new religious cults of our time, born in ignorance, nourished in sentimentality, and flourishing most vigorously in their natural habitat of Los Angeles. Most of these cults seem to have discovered two kinds of things: things that any reputable religionist knows already, and things that don't happen to be true. And so, because the founders of these systems are unaware of the past, they can render very little service in and to the present. It is highly relevant to note here that often, when modern irreligionists at last grow weary of their own negativity, and when they begin to search for a new and positive expression of life's meanings, they are readily trapped by just such marginal types of religious teaching. If thoughtfully they had examined the course of religious history, and thereby had come to understand the nature of religious change, they would not thus have been left naked to the enemies of all good sense.

In religion, and in the whole life that religion seeks to interpret and to evaluate, we need to be delivered at once from fear of what is new, and from contempt of what is old. Since religion is a matter precisely of choosing values in life, the proper business of religion is to test both new and old in our own best possible value judgments. Nothing is either good or bad because it is ancient, and nothing is either bad or good because we just discovered it this morning.

Religion has changed with the times, and it must change, as the times of man give new means of access to truth, and new ways toward the apprehension of eternal meanings. It is the point of reference that does not change, and that makes religion endure: the point of reference which is essential truth, the point of reference which is persisting value, the point of reference which religion has called 'God.' Religion is a radical force in its concern to get at the roots of things, to discover just what the abiding values really are. And there is no contradiction between these two.

Let our friends then divest themselves of their first superstition, that religion has not changed since they gave up the particular form of religious expression which they met in their reluctant Sunday School days. Religion has grown at least as much as they have; and religion will help them to grow a great deal more if they will but give heed to the nature of its surging life. Perhaps the major datum for them to learn, at this immediate point, is that the most significant change in religious thinking which has occurred since their childhood has been one of a conscious return to a more authentic and a nobler past. What has occurred in American religious circles has been a vital rediscovery of some of the original emphases of the Hebrew-Christian tradition, and a consequent dropping of many incidentals that derived from sixteenth century Church quarrels and from eighteenth century American isolation. Religion today is in no stage of arrested development. It is high time that the vocal opponents of religion should show cause that the same rightly may be said of them.

SUPERSTITION NO. 2

*that we can understand our cultural heritage
without knowledge of our religious traditions*

⊂Ξ The preceding chapter has made its plea for a more accurate knowledge of religious history, to the particular end that
permanence and change shall be seen each in its own true character. There are other reasons, as well, for acquaintance with the details of our religious past; and some of these need now to be examined against the background of irreligious superstition No. 2.
This particular rejection of scientific method perhaps is more
often implicit than articulate, but it is not therefore the less
real and mighty. The irreligious think to get along without
knowledge of the world's religious traditions because in effect
they have got along without such knowledge to date. Our present enquiry is designed to find out how much they have lost by
this particular deprivation.

It is usual, at least in matters of the intellect if not in the world
of material things, for one to undervalue what he himself does not
possess. Ignorant as they are of the details of the history of religion, today's irreligious people ignore also what religious history has done to them and for them. This manifestly is superstition of the crassest sort, for it is the blind acceptance of some
of life's principal determining phenomena without the making
of any effort to understand their true nature and their effective

force. The genuinely scientific mind can remain satisfied in no such obscurity; and the authentically scientific voice will speak only when the mind behind it has been adequately informed and trained.

Unhappily much of the fault in this area is to be charged directly to the spokesmen of one-sided and therefore incomplete religion. If the members of our present generation of the religiously illiterate went in their childhood to typical Protestant Sunday Schools, they probably were subjected to teachers whose only qualifying examination had been the oral question, '*Won't you take the class?*' Under these conditions it no doubt is true that often the children were given (as repeatedly now they assure us) not bread but a stone. If in their adolescence these already deprived were enrolled in public high schools and state universities, in California or in any one of a number of other states in the Union, they were cut off from any classroom contact whatever with those religious traditions which bulk most largely in our own West European culture. In either case, it was the dominance of limited and unhistoric religious views, among professedly religious people, that chiefly was to blame for the present mental darkness alike of unbelievers and of many who think they believe.

There is evidence that so far as the Churches are concerned, a new respect for sound learning is making itself effective in the materials and the methods of the religious teaching that is done by religious institutions. The requirement by all the 'standard' denominations that their clergy shall survive four years of college, and three years of graduate study in a seminary thereafter, means that the ministry of the Church increasingly reflects acquaintance with scientific method as a necessary technique, and with sound theological and Biblical scholarship as substance of doctrine. For the children and young people of the local parish each of the major Churches is publishing educational materials that are psychologically adapted to the various age levels, and that grow out of the accurate learning and the rigorous thinking of these Churches' greatest teachers. We may have hope not only that the present generation of pupils will learn more in Sunday School than their parents did, but also, and correlatively, that they will like it better and respect it more highly.

The graver weakness of today, and the persisting one, is in our public education, which in trying to be non-sectarian quickly became non-Christian, and so in total impact often anti-religious. Nor may we place the first responsibility for the secularizing of public education otherwhere than on those who have insisted on identifying religion with their own respective sectarianisms. A major vacuum exists in the educational opportunities of American young people: a vacuum which has been created because too many people were too sure that none but they should be permitted to fill it.

Literal Biblicism here has been the principal assassin of sound and rounded learning. If a teacher of history was not permitted to treat an Old Testament narrative as a normal historical document, checking it for accuracy and weighing it as to prejudice, he had no choice but to limit his ancient history sources to Egyptian, Babylonian, Assyrian, Greek, and Roman materials, which carried no odor of sanctity, and which therefore might be freely questioned and rationally used. If a teacher of literature might not exhibit the Psalms as imaginative poetry, nor a teacher of philosophy present Job as profoundly sincere philosophical groping, philosophy and literature simply had to be taught without reference to Job and the Psalms.

When in the 1920's Fundamentalism seized upon a number of state legislatures, the warfare between religion and science seemed openly to be declared, and for many on both sides there was no peace envisaged save one of unconditional surrender by the enemy. The Scopes 'monkey' case in Tennessee, which received the most publicity, unquestionably prevented many scientists from ever again according Christianity any sort of intellectual respect. (Few of them ever heard, of course, that the one University President in the state who spoke out openly against the 'anti-evolution' law was Arlo Ayres Brown of the Methodist University of Chattanooga.) A more engaging though less famous sample was that of the state assemblyman in another Southern commonwealth who introduced a measure providing that teachers of mathematics in tax-supported institutions should treat the value of *pi* not as 3.14159 but as 3.00, because the Chronicler says that Solomon 'made a molten sea of ten cubits from brim to brim, round in compass . . . and a line of thirty cubits did compass it round about.' Can one wonder if some math. teachers in that state skipped church the next Sunday?

Akin to Biblicism on the Protestant side has been ecclesiasticism on the Roman Catholic. Just as the local Fundamentalist group protested if a teacher on any academic level ventured to apply the standards of reasonable literary, historical, or scientific criticism to the Bible, so also the local Catholic community made life difficult for any teacher who was measurably objective about the history of the Church in the late Middle Ages and the Renaissance. The only practical way out of this dilemma, in which first one and then another religious system demanded exemption from any dispassionate and critical study, seemed to be the way we took: namely, to leave these religious systems without academic recognition of any kind.

But to explain this situation is neither to condone nor to accept it. It is as if the chemist were forbidden to include in his course outline any reference to the salts, or the botanist were required to be completely silent about conifers. Salts and conifers remain in the world, and the scientist who takes no account of them is neither a genuine scientist nor a complete person. It is no more possible to be a civilized member of our own society without reference to the religious elements which have gone into the building of our world.

Hebraism as well as Hellenism, the religious as well as the secular, are integral to the cultural pattern within which every one of us has grown up. There is no reason why half of our heritage, and the motivating half, should remain for ever unexplored. It happens that many of the religious leaders of today have made exploration newly possible because themselves they have learned to explore: which is one of the changes from former custom that the irreligious don't know about, and that therefore they attempt to deny. The next step is for all those who inevitably are affected by religious history, and that includes all of us, to start an honest enquiry into its nature and meaning as a determinant of our own total culture.

Do we think to discuss ideas? The history of philosophy has been assumed to be a permissible field for enquiry, so long as philosophy stayed far enough away from those crucial issues which belong to the philosophy of religion. Consequently the world views of Anaximander and Democritus and Heraclitus were taught and learned, and the value judgments of Plato and Aristotle, of the Stoics and the Epicureans. Then a great gulf was fixed, until secularism supervened in philosophy from the eighteenth century onward. Did not St. Augustine have a world view? Was St. Thomas Aquinas devoid of significant value judgments? Oh, but these were religious men, and theologians; and so it was inferred that what they thought was irrelevant to the growth of European thinking.

Yet the saints of Hippo and Aquino are at least as alive today, in the assumptions and the attitudes of all members of Western society, as are Zeno and Lucretius. The difference is that the thinking of the Christian philosophers, being commonly uncredited to them, is diffused into general overtones, and so is neither rightly appreciated nor soundly criticized. The divorcement of philosophy from theology has been, as is the case in all divorces, a tragic loss for both. Until the intellectual marriage is restored, and religion is readmitted to its rightful place in the household of human thought, there can be for us no adequate understanding of the vital forces that gave us our intellectual birth.

In the field of literature we have been quaintly and destructively inconsistent. It was pretty difficult to leave out Dante Alighieri and John Milton and John Bunyan from the catalogue of major European authors, and so we kept them in at least *pro forma*. There did arise, however, a prevailing judgment that they were pretty boring, and that because they were essentially religious writers. What had happened was that already we had expunged from the curriculum the basic materials which Dante and Milton and Bunyan had used, and so that mostly when we read them we had not the faintest idea what they were talking about. Today the case of T. S. Eliot is creating grave difficulty for secularists who dare not deny his power as a poet, yet who hate his judgments so fiercely that not uncommonly they transfer their hatred to the man. Again one suspects that the real difficulty is that they understand neither the man nor the materials with which he works.

It is not so generally realized that our 'secular' authors, too, were nourished upon Biblical and Churchly tradition, and took for granted its knowledge among their readers. Of course the Wife of Bath's prologue is read today for reasons quite other than its Biblical content; but the staggering inability of the average college Junior to understand readily what Chaucer is talking about arises directly from his bleak ignorance of data which for Chaucer were commonplace, and the knowledge of which he thought altogether appropriate for a not very devout laywoman of an English town in his day. Shakespeare, as a child of the Renaissance, has been considered wholly secular in his attitudes; yet Shakespeare not only indulges in Biblical allusions that have to be elaborately footnoted for a modern Sophomore, but also reproduces (as my colleague Elizabeth Pope has shown so brilliantly in her study of *Measure for Measure*) very much of the theological thinking of his time.

If we turn our attention to the study of English prose style, we find the teacher of literature required to take account of the lasting influence of the 'King James' version and the *Book of Common Prayer* (I suspect the latter even more than the former) upon the vocabulary and phrasing of every important writer of English for the next three centuries. Even if today we prefer, as the custom of some is, to write our learned treatises in polysyllabic gobbledygook, or if we fly to the other extreme of the language of the tavern or of the headline writer, we yet are disqualified for the informed discussion and the full appreciation of the former clear and ordered manner of statement in English, until we relate it aright to the direct and creative and vital expression of those who made the Scriptures and the Liturgy available to England in 'a language understanded of the people.' How can a modern youngster be expected to make headway through the periods of Carlyle and Macaulay when he is denied all acquaintance with their models? Yet that is just what has been forced upon us, first by those who took religion seriously but in the wrong way, and now by those who will not take religion seriously at all.

Let us journey next through Europe, on a summer vacation's tour with an American college student trained in our stubborn secularity. Thomas Cook and the American Express decree that he shall visit, for the sake of his artistic experience and appreciation, the galleries and the cathedrals. What does he see? No more than he is qualified to see; and our non-religious education has done its worst to keep him from seeing at all. To begin with, why the cathedrals? Or for that matter, why and how the beginnings of mediaeval art? If the student tourist knows no more of the Middle Ages than the structure of the feudal system, the rise of the Fuggers, and the wars of the barons, he never will understand the creative communal impulse that raised the towers of Chartres. If he is as blank about the book of Genesis as are most collegians, he can make but little out of Michelangelo.

When in Milan he looks above the doorway at the 'Last Supper' of Leonardo he will feel measurably at home, because of the chromos in shop windows on Main Street. He may even know (no thanks to his public school) what episode the painting represents. What can he possibly catch of its meaning, however, if he not only cannot identify the several apostles, but has no idea what parts respectively they played on that final evening of Jesus' ministry? And if then he looks at the numerous picturings of the 'harrowing of hell,' what is in his reach but grotesquerie if he is unaware of the Church's faith in its Lord's saving mission to all mankind, and in his triumph over all the forces of evil? To such a spiritual and intellectual starveling Susanna is only a lush nude, and Judith a grisly one. And so, by fearing to know religion, we have forbidden ourselves to know art.

Secularism has done us a like disservice as to music. This is not to say that all religious music has been good, or that secular music in itself is less than wholly valid. The critical necessity in musical understanding, however, and finally in musical performance as well, is that hearer and performer shall be able to share the respective thought worlds and emotional backgrounds of the composers. Acquaintance with eighteenth-century moods and manners long has been recognized to be essential to authentic interpretation of Haydn and Mozart, and realization of the nature of the romantic movement to sound assessment of Schubert and Tschaikowsky, even as some comprehension of Soviet politics to any meaningful acquaintance with the work of Shostakovich.

In precisely the same way, and as a part of the same requirement, the religious presuppositions and feelings of the makers of music, from Ambrosian and Gregorian chant through Palestrina to Bach, and on to Stravinsky, are integral alike to professional musical scholarship and to amateur appreciation. It is difficult enough, in these days of the disc jockey and the juke box, to inoculate young people with enthusiasm for the great musical tradition. We have made the task infinitely harder, whether as to securing attention in high-school music classes or in encouraging attendance at concerts, by wiping wholly blank the once full and exciting pages of the musicians' religious faith.

We need to remind ourselves, ever and again, not only that the beginnings of man's music were entirely religious, but also that the great music of our own heritage includes, besides symphonies and chamber works and operas, masses too and oratorios and settings of innumerable other sacred texts. The founders of European music, as we know it, were churchmen, and wrote for the Church. Bach was a church musician most of all, far more than he was the inventor of intricate harmonic forms. Haydn and Mozart composed masses as well as quartets and orchestral works, and so did Beethoven. Berlioz and Bruckner followed these, as in our own time Stravinsky and Poulenc. We do not understand Brahms without the German Requiem, nor Stravinsky without the Symphony of Psalms.

Most religious music inevitably is associated with words. Now words often are missed in the hearing of music, even when the words are in English. The use of a foreign language complicates things further, as witness the problem of operatic understanding in the United States. But with the opera it is customary at least to provide program synopses, and to make available bilingual libretti. Moreover, the typical opera plot, while scarcely probable in detail, moves in a secular world which is reasonably familiar to hearers both willing and unwilling.

In the case of religious music, where in the nature of the case many of the original verbal texts are in Latin, and another great block in German, there is added to the language barrier an even more opaque screen of spiritual incomprehension. Nor: presumably because religious meaning is supposed to be beyond the reach of modern students of music, and/or because it is thought to be irrelevant to musical enjoyment: do the purveyors of music help as easily they might. In the matter of recordings, for example, the highest quality of performance often is accompanied by the smallest concern for the hearer's full realization. A quick check of my own record collection shows that, for thirty major religious works, of which but seven are in English, the record companies have provided verbal texts in a total of just fifteen cases. The inference would seem to be that the words the music was written to convey are quite unimportant; and so that religious music has no religious meaning, or at all events no religious interest.

The 'concert' performances of masses, of Bach oratorios and cantatas, and of Jewish sacred services, too often make emphatic this lack of interest in the composers' intent. How can one appreciate the great masses, whether of the earlier centuries or of our own, without some recognition of what happens at the altar before, during, and after the 'set pieces' that chorus and soloists sing now in a wholly secular auditorium? How may one realize either the magnitude or the intensity of Bach's achievement without knowing not only Bach's involved duties in the Leipzig churches, but also the depth of his personal faith? How may one share in the musical realization of Ernst Bloch's service, or of Darius Milhaud's, unless one can share in the outward sorrows and the triumphant inner faith of the Jewish people throughout the ages?

The churches are at fault, of course, because so often they have surrendered the best of church music to the concert hall, and have inflicted on their congregations not only feeble performance but also banal selection. Nor may we claim that plainsong reveals its meaning and its power on first introduction: it is for this generation a taste that has to be acquired. But the reason that the taste has to be acquired is precisely that this generation is so pitifully unaware alike of the technical history of religious music and of the historic achievements of religious faith. The secularizing of our culture has impoverished music among musicians and among churchmen both; and something like the mediaeval cultural synthesis will have to be restored ere the Church can recapture its former musical glories, and before the world can grasp the treasures that the music of religion yet has available to give it.

It is not to be pretended that, in our modern culture, religious knowledge and understanding have the same kind of relevance in the domain of science as in the humanities and the arts. Science, we say and assume, is secular in its very nature. The rise of modern science synchronized with, whether or not it caused, the development of today's primarily secular point of view. Yet even here a word needs to be said to those who have made non-religious science their religion, lest in doing this they leave other important things undone.

As to science itself, the devout spirit of the unremitting quest for reality is in its own character profoundly religious. The scientist who sees only the dissected tissues on the slide, or worse, only the minutiae of other scientists' reporting in the journals, is unlikely to discover much of the larger pattern or to present his findings in any significant context. The greatest among the scientists are they who have imagination enough to envisage the connections between datum and datum, and thus to identify the coherence of phenomena as well as their particularities. This quest for greater meaning is one with the religious quest toward ultimate truth; and it is not to be achieved without what we must count a truly religious concern.

This does not mean, however, and never should be understood to mean, that the discoveries of science prove the truth of religion in general, or the existence of God in particular. Some of the scientists who personally are religious men here have fallen into a trap: for no other reason than that they have allowed themselves to be quite unscientific on the religious side. To put it bluntly, their inadequacy as theologians disqualifies them as scientific defenders of religion, however effectively they may demonstrate religious living in their own persons.

The 'proofs of God,' effectively refuted in philosophy, have not become proofs again in the laboratory. The realm of religion is the realm of faith, and specifically not that of demonstration, as I shall argue at some length in the chapter which follows this. It is science that needs the religious spirit, not religion a scientific proof. Science needs to have faith in the reliability of evidence, and the relatedness of phenomena, and the dependability of the observer's mind; and science, to be of creative use to man, needs also awareness of human values as well as precise measurements of physical objects. Irreligion will not contribute to these necessities of science, but vital religion will.

Beyond this, both scientist and layman require the arts and the humanities if they are to be complete persons. As we have seen, religion is one of the humanities, and religion also is an art and the creator of art forms. To leave religious awareness out of life not only reduces understanding of history, philosophy, and literature, of architecture, painting, and music, in the specific ways and at the specific points noted above. It also restricts appreciation even where the points of reference are not religious in the more narrowly technical sense.

Religion was not a side issue, nor even one among a number of categories, through most of the period in which our culture was taking form. It rather was the pervading atmosphere in which all men lived, and which inescapably they breathed. Thus it is essentially a false distinction which makes Botticelli's Madonna and his Venus (for both of which he seems to have used the same model) respectively Catholic and pagan, or the Missa Solemnis a religious work and the Ninth Symphony a secular one. The Florentine master was pagan and Catholic at once, and in complete personal integration. The Hymn to Joy is no less religious with Schiller's words in Carnegie Hall than it is with Van Dyke's in a Presbyterian Church. Indeed it is more effectively religious in so far as Schiller's is the better poetry, and Bob Shaw's choral group does the better singing. But the religion of this music is not wholly available to them who have avoided any experience of the religious uplifting of the human heart. Joy in the life that God has given us is religious whether reflected in pagan or in Christian symbols; but there can be no final joy for those who deny that life has such meaning as to make it joyful.

Thus religion is integral to our cultural history whether in the detail of religious expression, or in that enlargement of the human spirit which is religious fulfillment. By cutting off the knowledge of detail, this age of ours has denied meaning to thought, to books, to painting, to music. By abjuring the religious approach in general, it has denied ultimate meaning to human experience. Thus our culture has been drained of its very life blood, and its children have become puny and pallid bystanders, afraid to live as they have feared to believe.

We cannot know our historic heritage without knowing historic religion, and we cannot live in our heritage fully without breathing its vitalizing religious spirit. The contrary superstition has cost us much already, and it threatens to rob us of the power to gain hereafter. If the irreligious will be scholarly enough to study religion, they will appreciate more truly what we have. If they will be enquiring enough to test religion, they will begin to be qualified to give us yet more.

SUPERSTITION NO. 3

that religion is necessarily
at odds with fact and reason

⊂⊃ 'We have no religion,' said one of my wife's friends. 'My husband is a scientist.' The thesis of this chapter is simply that the lady's statement is an absolute *non sequitur*. That instead of this it seems to many to be a *sequitur* of inescapable cogency is unquestionably true, and provides the occasion for arguing the point.

There are two sorts of ground for adhering to the superstition that religion is contrary to reason, and necessarily at war with it. One is that through the centuries a vast number of quite irrational people, who have thought themselves to be religious and who indeed may have been so quite sincerely, have managed to identify their religion with their irrationality, their unreason with their faith. The other factor is that religion by its nature does venture, and must, into realms outside the reach of logical demonstration, and so beyond the limits of formal logic. Neither of these considerations, however, requires either religion to repudiate good sense, or clear thinking to hold religion in contempt.

The ignorance and irrationality of many faithful believers, while not to be denied, needs to be viewed historically and to be understood psychologically and sociologically. To begin with we must observe that precise knowledge and inexorable logic never have characterized the majority of humankind. Further, we must remember that the type of knowledge which we call 'scientific' has been available only for a couple of centuries. It is true that Aristotelian logic, admitted still to be intellectually respectable even if by some thought to be superseded, was current before the rise of Christianity. But the best of logical systems cannot hope to arrive at valid conclusions if its premises are faulty; and so the observations of science are basic to any finally adequate working out of a meaningful world view. Yet science is new; and logical thinking, with or without a scientific base, remains everywhere uncommon.

The question is superficially whether religious people have been appreciably less scientific, or characteristically more illogical, than the general run of men and women. Ultimately the important issue is whether religion intrinsically must negate science and must deny reason. Let us take the historic human case first, and the timeless philosophical one after it.

That the majority of churchgoers, even in our own time, are lamentably ill-informed and pathetically unreasonable is patently true. It is no less true, however, that the majority of patients neither know the mechanisms of their own physical health nor comprehend the processes of therapy. The vast number of litigants are ignoramuses as to what the law says, and everlasting nuisances to their attorneys as to how their cases should be argued. And any Sunday driver knows that everyone else on the road that afternoon is blissfully unaware of the traffic code and utterly stupid about turning at an intersection. Ignorance and stupidity are wellnigh universal marks of mankind; and they are no less prevalent in medicine, law, and transportation than they are in religion.

Yet we do not think to abjure physic and the physician because the herd doses itself with patent nostrums. We do not decide to return to anarchy because the law continually runs afoul of human cussedness and doltishness. We do not even stay at home because adolescents, nervous ladies, and drunks insist on sharing the streets and highways with us. Medicine yet can heal, and law control, and automobiles take us where we want to go. Is religion, even faulty religion, entitled to a like tolerance?

The curious element here is that the articulate irreligious of today, who are so acutely conscious of their own superiority to the Lumpenproletariat, insist that majority ignorance and unreason are implicitly to be trusted, alone are authoritative, in this sole field of religion. Rejecting the quack, the shyster, and the incompetent driver, as unfortunate but inevitable factors in the human scene, they rightly turn to the well-trained medico, to the learned counselor, to the skillful chauffeur and mechanic. Reason itself then requires that equally they shall evaluate religion not in its weakest manifestations, but in its strongest; not by its majority confusions but by its clarifying leadership; not by its popular failures but by its historic achievements.

When once this principle is investigated, tested, and established, it turns out that the warfare between reason and faith, or between science and religion, is no more than a colonial skirmish on the fringes of both domains, fought in general by those on both sides whose allegiance is uncertain and whose objectives are confused. That for most of the centuries of Christian history churchmen believed the earth to be flat and motionless is true. Thus also believed almost everyone else, for there was known no compelling evidence to the contrary. That religious people believed in physical miracles, without adequate supporting evidence, is clear from the records. It is no less clear that many non-religious people still are convinced of unprovable and often of disprovable manifestations.

If it be argued that religion was active and sometimes violent in its opposition to new scientific ideas, this also is to be granted; but it too inspires an immediate *tu quoque*. The majority of astronomers in the sixteenth and seventeenth centuries were no more pleased with Copernicus and Galileo than was the Church. The great mass of doctors denied Harvey's evidence for the circulation of the blood. The almost unanimous voice of 'naturalists' (there scarcely were any biologists then) heaped scorn upon the observations and the gently presented inferences of Darwin. The Church, therefore, when it rejected new discoveries, was reflecting the prevailing mood of the times at least as much as the nature of religion; and more so if religion be seen in its true historic character.

Much of recent controversy has turned upon the issue of evolution. Even today, in some regions, it is supposed both by church people and by the unchurched that this is an irreconcilable conflict. 'But of course you don't believe in evolution,' said a school teacher (not a Mills alumna) to our Summer Session Chaplain at Mills College. 'Why not?' he asked in some bewilderment. 'Well, you're a minister, aren't you?' Even more recently, a month before this writing, a student in a state college hurled at a Rabbi and myself the challenge, 'Would either of you go for evolution in any form?'

My answer, in which the Rabbi fully concurred, was that I would 'go' first for evolution in the religious views of creation as I find them presented in the Scriptures: for evolution from one of them into the other. It is a commonplace of Biblical scholarship, though it may be still a secret hidden from most of the irreligious, that the first two chapters of the book of Genesis contain two independent accounts of the creation of the world, and that Chapter ii antedates Chapter i by at least five hundred years. What happened in the centuries between?

In the tenth century B.C. the Israelites scarcely had passed out of nomadism, and their world view was restricted to the nearest and the simplest items of experience. Accordingly the earlier account of the creation is as naïve as were its writers. The earth itself is taken quite for granted, and *a fortiori* the heavens and all that in them is. We hear only of the creation of man, of plants and animals, and finally of the mysterious creature called woman. These things the early story-tellers knew, and these they wrote about.

In the fifth century the Jews were under Persian rule, and for long years had been exposed to Babylonian culture. The result appears in the later creation story, that of Genesis i. Here the universe is seen through Babylonian eyes, and the work of God is presented as the building of a Babylonian cosmos. Even its chronology reflects the sexagesimal system of Babylon. From the point of view of Albert Einstein, Babylonian cosmology and mathmatics no doubt are inadequate; but they represent the best scientific approaches within the reach of the Jews of that day, and those Jews did not hesitate to integrate the newly learned science with their fathers' faith. I shall not belabor the point that Dr. Einstein seems to find that faith yet tenable, in the cosmos which he himself has done most to reveal to this generation.

'But,' says the persistent disbeliever, 'your great Christian teachers denied reason, and glorified obscurantism.' Then hastily he quotes *Credo quia absurdum,* 'I believe because it is ridiculous,' and *Credo ut intelligam,* 'I believe in order that I may understand.' He has not yet given me, nor have I found, an authentic early source for the former. There is, however, a comparable saying in Tertullian's *De carne Christi*: 'It is certain because it is impossible.' But one should note that Tertullian wrote this work after his expulsion from the Church as a heretic; and that it was just in the irrationality of Tertullian's Montanism that the Church identified his heretical bent.

The other saying, *Credo ut intelligam,* is an authentic expression of eleventh-century orthodoxy, being from the writings of St. Anselm, one of the great Archbishops of Canterbury. But it requires careful analysis before it will yield its fulness of meaning. 'I believe in order that I may understand.' The whole issue between faith and reason, then, turns on the nature of what one means when he says, 'I believe.'

The first difficulty that faces us here is that of the poverty of language: specifically, of the differing but equally serious poverties of Greek, Latin, and English. The problem in English is reflected by the small boy's use of 'faith' in the definition, 'Faith is believing things that ain't so,' and in the White Queen's famous feat of believing 'as many as six impossible things before breakfast.' Here both 'faith' and 'believing' are used in the same sense: in the strictly limited sense of intellectual credence. We do have in English the noun 'belief' accompanying the verb 'to believe'; but we have no verb at all to correspond with our noun 'faith.' The Latin situation is comparable, with *credo* as 'I believe' and *fides* as 'faith,' but with the one lacking a cognate noun and the other an associated verb.

Greek is in a sense even poorer yet, but by the same token it is a bit less confusing. There is in Greek only one root in this area: and so only a single noun, *pistis*, which variously we translate 'faith' or 'belief.' The related verb, *pisteuo*, we have to render 'I believe' in all cases, because we have in English no such expression as 'I faith'; and so, in English and Latin as well, we get in general not better than half the meaning that is conveyed in the Greek verb.

One New Testament document does indeed treat *pistis* and *pisteuo* in the narrowest possible sense of 'belief,' or 'I believe.' That is the epistle of St. James, for whose author *pistis* signifies nothing other than intellectual opinion. 'Thou believest that God is one?' he challenges. 'Thou doest well. So do the demons, and they shudder.' With such a definition taken for granted, this early Christian writer cannot but conclude that 'belief,' or 'faith' as he conceives it, is a very secondary matter; and so that true religion is to be found rather in 'works,' which he defines in terms of social concern and personal integrity.

Now St. James' definitions are easy and obvious, and his simple gospel of decent behavior appeals immediately to every one of us. What Christians and non-Christians alike have to realize is that not all Christian writers used these easy and obvious definitions, and that not all Christian thinkers have found entire contentment in this highly simplified gospel. There is for example the difficult declaration in St. Paul's epistle to the Romans, 'To him that worketh not, but believeth on him that justifieth the ungodly, his faith is counted for righteousness.' If into this declaration of St. Paul we put St. James' definition of belief or faith as mere opinion, we get something deadly indeed: 'To him that does not lead a Christian life, but holds the right opinions, his opinion is counted for righteousness.'

Unhappily the view that this is actual Christian doctrine has been current not only among those who think Christians are by nature gullible, but also among many who think they are Christian themselves, and who by maintaining this position announce their own gullibility. This is the position, and this the tragic fallacy, of 'Fundamentalism.' Supposing faith to be opinion, and holding among their other opinions one to the effect that every word of the Bible is literal and infallible truth, the Fundamentalists have concluded that salvation rests upon man's holding of the right intellectual views. Here, of course, they have flatly ignored St. James, whose doctrine was at least better than his semantics. They have done even worse violence to St. Paul, who by 'works' meant Jewish ceremonial, and by 'faith' personal commitment of life.

It has been such Fundamentalism, an uninformed but militant devotion to opinion for opinion's sake, that has led so many people, inside the Church and outside, to suppose that religion is opinion; and in general untenable, impossible, absurd opinion. If such a definition of religion or of Christianity be correct, and with it the definition of faith merely as a series of rigid intellectual formulae, then Christians are gullible indeed, and religion is hopelessly at odds with reason and with facts. But this is not the historic nature of Christianity, and this is not what normative Christianity ever has conceived to be the true nature of true faith.

What we have to do is to press the matter of definition further. Three words, which too often are confused, must sharply be distinguished one from another. They are, respectively, 'faith,' 'opinion,' and 'knowledge.'

Knowledge belongs to the realm of demonstrable fact. 'I know,' I may say, 'that the correct chemical formula for water is H_2O, because once I manufactured some water in the laboratory by combining hydrogen and oxygen in the proportions of two to one.' 'I know it was very cold this last week' is a permissible remark; but it is the more legitimate if we have based it on thermometer readings than if we are simply reporting our impressions of a ground-floor classroom at eight o'clock on a winter morning. Knowledge relates to fact; and the more surely the fact can be established by laboratory techniques and procedures, the firmer the resultant knowledge is.

Opinion also pertains to the realm of fact, but of fact which is not so readily susceptible to absolute proof. Thus it is my opinion, as a loyal Californian, that we shall not have much rain in California between June 1 and October 1 of next year; but I cannot test that opinion till next summer comes. What is a matter of opinion at one time thus may become a matter of certain knowledge later on.

In the same way, what is a matter of knowledge for one person may be necessarily a matter of opinion for another. When a scientist reports to me a series of his experiments, and the inferences he has drawn from them, I assume the correctness of his view on the basis of his report, and on that of his standing as a scientist; but I personally am in no position to prove or to disprove it. On the other hand, I do know that the epistle of St. James uses in its vocabulary over 90% of words that are of classical Greek origin. I know, because I have counted the words and have checked their earlier appearances. I would assume that this datum, which is fact to my personal knowledge, would be in the realm of opinion, at best, for most natural scientists; and what they supposed to be true about the Greek vocabulary of St. James would depend upon their not too demonstrable opinion of my status as a student of the New Testament.

Knowledge and opinion then operate in the area of fact; and the distinction between them inheres in the degree of proof possible or actually achieved. What is the relationship of faith to these? Correctly understood, faith does not operate in the area of fact at all; and so in that area it leaves us of necessity to deal with knowledge and opinion. Since religion makes contacts with all of life, it never is permitted to leave opinion and knowledge out of account; and in their fields religion must accept their methods and their criteria. Thus the knowledge of a Copernican universe works havoc upon opinions holding to a physical heaven and hell; a knowledge of biology forbids us to think that *homo sapiens* was created complete in a twenty-four hour day some six thousand years ago; and the knowledge of historical documents may do much to modify our opinions about the history of Christian thinking.

Where knowledge is available, knowledge must be sought: and that by knowledge's own proper techniques of scientific method. Pending proof, we are permitted to hold opinions in the realm of fact. Faith cannot contravene established fact, and faith has no right to dispute reasonable opinion: for these are not the realms in which faith lives and works. To say 'I believe in evolution' is scarcely a more sensible remark than to declare 'I don't believe in evolution'; for evolution is a matter of a reasonable judgment founded upon exact knowledge, and not at all an appropriate object of anyone's 'believing.' The subject matter of faith is to be sought otherwhere, and the life of faith lives otherwise.

The realm of religious faith is the realm of values, and values are by their nature not subject to scientific demonstration. (Perhaps we might except 'economic value'; but even here there is a very large subjective element involved.) Religious people now and then have thought to carry their faith over into the zone of fact and opinion, as already we have seen; and the world has seen that almost invariably these supposed spokesmen for religion then have been ingloriously driven from the field. Conversely, however, scientists sometimes have thought to invade the realm of religion with the methods and the criteria of science; and when they have done this, they have been trespassing just as improperly.

When the scientist, having determined by geological investigation that some of our rock formations are millions of years old, declares that he has shown the Bible to be nonsense, he is talking nonsense himself; and that because he is being completely unscientific about the Bible's literary origins and its essential character. When, having examined the embryos of snakes and humans and having found them closely similar, a biologist ventures to conclude that this shows that God made neither human nor snake, he is just as far outside the field in which he is qualified to express a judgment. Much of the breath that is being spent in modern controversy about religion would immediately be saved if once we could get clear this distinction between the realm of scientific knowledge and that of religious faith. The two zones simply are separate, and in their ways of approach they do not overlap at all.

Faith certainly is not 'believing things that ain't so'; but very often it is just believing things that do not seem to be so, and always it is believing what cannot be proved to be so. The classic definition of faith remains that of the writer of the epistle to the Hebrews: that 'faith is . . . the conviction of things not seen.' There are no scientific proofs of the existence of God, or of the divinity of the Christ, or of the inspiration of the Bible, or of the immortality of the human spirit; but neither, when these values are rightly understood, can there be scientific disproof of them. Such problems as these are matters not of scientific demonstration, but of value judgment. That is to say, they are matters of faith properly so called.

We cannot prove, either in laboratory terms or by syllogisms, that God exists. We cannot establish by the scientific method even that the sayings of Jesus are accurately quoted, let alone that they have enduring validity. (In *fact*, of course, we can prove that Jesus' sayings were very casually and variously reported by the Gospel writers and editors.) We cannot demonstrate that man carries within himself anything but the seeds of his own destruction. It is doubtful whether by evidence and logical argument we can guarantee even the rightness of our most common human attitudes of goodwill, and concern for others, and simple honesty of word and behavior. These are not matters of knowledge. Therefore and thereby, and because though indemonstrable they are important, they become matters of faith and so matters of religion.

To say that we believe in God is something neither based on scientific evidence nor contrary to it. It is simply a choice of faith in a wholly different realm; and it is faith whether the choice be positive or negative. To say that Jesus is the Christ is the expression of a judgment about Jesus: and one that depends finally both upon our defining the term 'Christ' so that it has a meaning on which we can agree, and upon the individual's decision as to whether that category is one that he himself finds significant. To say that the Bible is inspired is to record not an opinion about its literal veracity, but an experience of its effective inspiring of our own spirits. To say that man is immortal is a matter of knowing what we mean by immortality, and then of deciding whether in terms of that meaning we are willing to risk these mortal lives of ours for the unproved values which by faith we have chosen.

In his little book called *A Student in Arms*, written while he was a soldier in the trenches of France during World War I, Donald Hankey defined religion as 'betting your life there is a God.' That says it for us, if only our concept of God is large enough and living enough. Religion is precisely betting our lives that our chosen values, admittedly indemonstrable, nevertheless are worth our living by and our dying for. Religion is committing ourselves to those values which we have chosen, without reservation, without hesitation, without thought of retreat.

Just because we can readily see and know some things, they are the easier and therefore the lesser things of life. The great ones, the finally determinative ones, always are beyond the reach of sight and knowledge. Always they have to be in the realm of faith. The religious person, including the value of honesty among those to which he is committed, will avail himself of all the knowledge that the scientist can supply, of all the facts he can learn, and of all the hard thinking he can do. Beyond all this, the religious person will give himself in fidelity to the faith that he has made his own, and therein he will find the completeness of his living. 'The just shall live by faith,' accurately translated and not merely paraphrased, is to be read simply, 'The good man lives by his fidelity.'

'I believe in order that I may understand.' How, apart from faith, is man to understand himself? How without faith can he hope to understand what is happening to him today? How else shall he find values adequate to counter the denials which life so violently hurls at him? St. Anselm had his problems too; and for him as for us it was faith, not opinion, that was basic to understanding.

The supposed conflict between science and religion, between reason and faith, always has been needless and therefore always has been needlessly expensive. It is more than ever tragic in this day, when confusion is all about us and within most of us. Science indeed has upset much of former religious opinion, and world chaos has done more to challenge personal stability. The answer is not to be found in a debate between religion and science. It is rather to be sought in the joint service of science and religion to man who needs them both.

Science is the intellectual orderer of chaos, discerning patterns of relationship and working out the observable sequences of cause and effect. Religion is the moral orderer of chaos, reminding us that there are perduring values in the realm of the spirit, calling us ever to loyalty to our best, whatever the outer challenges or the visible returns may be. Religion and science are not at odds. They are allies, mutually necessary and complementary allies, in the warfare of all mankind against ignorance on the one hand and against neurosis on the other. Science will give us knowledge of the facts, but there it must stop. Religion, depending on science in the realm of fact, dares us and encourages us to press on into the realm of value. It is only superstition, ignorant both of the facts of religion and of its values, that will think to sever this union of the disciplined mind and the courageous heart.

SUPERSTITION NO. 4

that religion is not a
valid field of scholarship

◖◗ This chapter is something of an afterthought, since it was not included in my list of irreligious superstitions as first I drew it up. But there is plenty of evidence that this particular superstition, that religion is not a respectable field of academic enquiry, is widely current: and especially among members of college and university faculties. A biologist colleague of mine, forced by professional courtesy to hear my report on some work I had been doing about the origins and development of the Apostles' Creed, came up to me at the end. 'George,' he said, 'I had no idea it was possible to be scientific about religion.' Many others, I fear, have no such idea yet. It is high time they got the idea.

It is because it is so important sharply to distinguish between the scientific concern with knowledge and the religious quest for faith, as we have just been noticing the difference, that now it is desirable to pause long enough to identify the ways in which exact scholarship may be relevant to the field of religion. The thoughtful religionist rightly will insist that religion finally is supra-scientific and supra-rational, and therefore that its findings are not to be judged by factual and logical criteria only. At the same time he will remind himself, and his hearers, that many of the phenomena of religion, belonging by their nature to the phenomenal, factual world, always must be submitted to precise

: *43*

observation and critical analysis before their character can be known or their significance assessed.

Religion is not science; but there are very large areas in which it is possible, and therefore mandatory, to be completely scientific about religion. The former types of difficulty here are evident again: first, that many religious people have refused ever to be scientific about anything; and, second, that many non-religious people have managed completely to ignore the tremendous mass of careful, scholarly work that has been done in the field of religion. The thesis of this section is that religion is, and of right ought to be, an academic discipline fully worthy to stand beside any of the others that are listed in our college and university catalogues. Sample pieces of the evidence, though samples only, will follow.

Literary criticism is as relevant to the text of the Bible as to that of Shakespeare; and its achievements here have been not less significant, not less disciplined, not less revealing, in Biblical studies than in Elizabethan. The beginnings of the story are ancient indeed. The very arrangement of the Bible in Hebrew reflects the critical judgment of the Rabbis of the Council of Jamnia, held in A.D. 96, to the effect that Daniel was not one of the historic prophets, and that the books of Chronicles provided less dependable history than did those of Samuel and Kings. Again, the making of the standard Masoretic text of the Hebrew scriptures, while undoubtedly it preserved some late misreadings, indicates full awareness, on the part of Jewish scholars a few centuries later, that the existing manuscripts were faulty and needed critical analysis and reconstruction.

In another connection we have noted that a number of the leading early Christians held views of Biblical authorship and intent which no modern Fundamentalist could bring himself to accept. To the names already mentioned we should add at least those of the Christian Platonists of Alexandria, who worked long and conscientiously on the problems of authorship and literary connections. St. Clement almost certainly erred when he ascribed the epistle to the Hebrews to St. Paul (a theory no one had suggested earlier); but Clement's intellectual honesty could not identify the Greek style as Paul's, and so he offered the hypothesis that St. Luke had done the translation from a Semitic (Hebrew or Aramaic) original. St. Clement's even more learned successor, Origen, repudiated his teacher's Pauline theory, and after examining all the possibilities concluded very frankly that 'only God knows' who wrote the epistle.

We have seen also that the early and great Protestant reformers applied decidedly critical judgment to the technical details involved in the study of Biblical materials. It is worth recording here, anent the letter to the Hebrews, that Martin Luther originated one of the most reasonable of nominations of a possible author: that is, Apollos of Alexandria, who seems to have had precisely the combination of Christian faith with a Philonic, Jewish-Greek background that the epistle reflects. 'Only God knows' remains the final answer as to who wrote the work; but Luther's suggestion is much more than a random and unsupported guess.

Renaissance and Reformation together brought about renewed and intensified scholarly examination of the Scriptures. Erasmus, editing the New Testament in Greek for its first printing, found himself driven to evaluate the relatively few but quite variant manuscripts to which he had access, and to choose among their readings. Thus he laid the foundation for the vast work of the 'lower,' or textual, criticism that has been going on ever since. Today the number of known Greek manuscripts of the New Testament, complete or partial, and pre-Gutenberg in their origin, is well over five thousand; and since no two of them are quite identical, the task of determining the earliest and most accurate texts is subtle, demanding, and never ending. Constantine Tischendorf's seventh edition, published in 1869–72, was an epochal achievement; but many of its judgments now have been superseded as new discoveries have been made and new patterns of relationship worked out.

Parenthetically we may observe that some of the unpopularity of modern Biblical translations arises from the fact that critical comparison of manuscripts has forced the excision from the text of many familiar and sometimes highly controversial passages. Among these are the last twelve verses of St. Mark's Gospel, which are lacking from most of the earlier and more dependable copies; the reference to the angel who 'troubled' the water of the pool of Bethesda, in St. John v, an item which has even less support in early manuscript witness; and the explicit statement of the doctrine of the Holy Trinity in I St. John v, which appears actually in one Greek manuscript only, and that a very late one. The issue here, let it be remembered, is not at all whether one believes or disbelieves what the disputed passages say. It is simply whether scholarly judgment can regard them as belonging to the authentic originals as they came from the authors' hands: and so it is an issue of scholarship in the strictest sense.

The so-called 'higher' criticism (an unfortunate term, since it lent itself to attacks as being high handed if not high hat) deals with the authorship, dates, and purposes of the Biblical writings. I shall mention here, quickly to set it aside, the silly notion that 'the lower criticism believes in the Bible, and the higher criticism doesn't.' In the same category is the supposition that there ever was any such creature as a 'higher critic.' The adjective applies to the field of enquiry, not to the man nor to the views which he may have reached; and it serves simply to distinguish the 'higher' problems of authorship and intent from the 'lower' ones of verbal reproduction.

In this 'higher' field there has been worked out, chiefly in the last century and a half, a general consensus held by the entire world of what may be regarded as 'standard' Biblical study. Among its unanimously accepted conclusions is that of the composite character of the Pentateuch, the so-called 'books of Moses.' Here the separation of interwoven documentary sources has been carried out in the greatest detail, and with such cogency that there is no substantial dissent among scholars who have labored on the problem. An easily available presentation of the pattern is that provided by James Moffatt's *The Holy Bible: A New Trans-*

lation, in which for the first five books of the Old Testament the principal documents are distinguished by variations in typography. The layman will find a beautiful sample chapter in Exodus xiv, a mosaic (the pun is irresistible) of three originally independent accounts of the crossing of the Red Sea, written over a span of at least five hundred years.

Each of these constituent elements of the books as we know them has been dated, by the use of linguistic and historical evidence both internal and external, with at least as much accuracy as has been achieved for the works of Homer and Hesiod. The same type of analysis, applied to the Old Testament books other than the first five, has shown that essentially the same documentary strands run through all the 'historical' works, and that each presents its own consistent interests and emphases in its own consistent literary style. Similarly most of the books of the prophets turn out, upon scrutiny, to be in their present form compilations of materials from various hands and written at various times.

The present book of Amos, for example, includes probably authentic sayings of the eighth-century herdsman from the wilderness of Tekoa, but also many interpolations, and a long optimistic addendum which totally contravenes the original prophet's point of view, but which is fully appropriate as a word of hope during the years of the Babylonian exile two centuries later. 'Isaiah' brings together the work of two major figures living a hundred and fifty years apart, plus many fragments written between the times of the two and after that of the second. The first three chapters of Micah are authentic words of a small farmer of Southwestern Judah in the early seventh century, the rest later additions. It is not necessary here to catalogue all the prophetic works. Suffice it to say that the same sort of careful, critical, dispassionate, and productive labor has been done, and still is being done, on all of them.

In the case of the Psalms, literary criticism has made it practically certain that the great majority belong to periods long after that of David, and that at least a few date from the time of the Maccabees, in the second century B.C. Ecclesiastes turns out to be an originally pessimistic essay which has undergone two processes of interpolation, one by a rather dull proverb-compiler and the other by an eager defender of a more cheerful Jewish orthodoxy. The book of Job includes at least four major literary sources: the original folk-tale, the pessimistic symposium built upon it, the 'Elihu' chapters which try rather feebly to resolve the symposium's doubts, and the 'voice from the whirl-wind,' which sets the doubts against the inscrutable background of the whole universe. Finally an editor who had missed the entire point tacked on the old 'happy ending' of the folk-tale, thus completely confusing the issue as Job and his friends had dis-cussed it.

This may perhaps be the appropriate point to comment on the sad results, in many a department of English or of World Litera-ture, of the general ignorance of Biblical scholarship which pre-vails in the secular world. Many courses in 'The Bible as Litera-ture,' though given full academic credit and accorded unques-tioning campus recognition, are pitifully inadequate from the point of view of sound learning. I have reference here not to slop-piness on the part of retired clergy who are pressed into service in small colleges, though such sloppiness exists. I am speaking rather of Professors of English, in particular, who think to treat the Bible simply as a Jacobean English document, and who blandly ignore the whole and critically important substratum of the original languages, the intricate problems of the relation-ships of the original sources, and the historical backgrounds and intellectual presuppositions of the original authors. This secular approach to religion as an academic study has been, in many in-stances, the reverse of scholarly; and only the religious scholars can supply the data of which the non-religious have proved themselves so pathetically although so proudly innocent.

As to the New Testament, about which the non-religious know as little but usually say less, literary investigation has done the same kind of exacting work and has produced the same kind of decisive results. St. Mark's Gospel is recognized as a substantially independent document of about A.D. 65. St. Matthew's and St. Luke's are composites dating from about the end of the first century, and each of them embodying within it almost all of the text of St. Mark. The Fourth Gospel, finally, is a Greek-oriented philosophical restatement written not earlier than A.D. 110, and almost certainly not by the apostle St. John.

Nine of the letters traditionally attributed to St. Paul preserve their authenticity in the light of rigorous enquiry, but (along with Hebrews) the letters to the Ephesians, and to Timothy and Titus, are to be assigned to later Christian hands. (Ephesians and II Timothy, however, seem to include genuine Pauline materials, in the former case borrowed directly from the authentic epistle to the Colossians.) Probably none of the so-called 'General Epistles' were written by the apostles whose names they bear; and in this judgment the scholars of today find themselves in agreement with many of the Church Fathers of the third and fourth centuries. The Book of Revelation is seen as one of the typical apocalypses of Hellenistic Judaism, borrowing much of its detail from Daniel and from other late Jewish sources, but dealing with Christian problems under Roman rule rather than with Jewish sufferings under the successors of Alexander the Great.

Literary criticism has made possible an equally critical approach, and an equally significant achievement, in the field of history. The wanderings of the Israelite tribes, if traced through the earliest sources, appear to be normal nomadic experience. The 'conquest of Canaan' is revealed as scarcely a conquest at all, but rather an interpenetration of the Israelite and Canaanite peoples, pastoral and agricultural respectively. The Philistines, those stock enemies of every adult Israelite and the bogeymen of every child in Israel, are by historical enquiry rehabilitated somewhat as to character and intelligence, and overwhelmingly as to political and military success. The internal and external politics of Israel and Judah come clear as we succeed in placing the documentary evidence aright, both in the narratives of Samuel-Kings and Chronicles, which are secondary authorities, and in the vigorous political campaigning and pamphleteering of the prophets, whose surviving works are our primary sources.

In the same way, again, the life of Jesus and the history of the early Church have had to be worked out by identifying the dates of documents, by comparing one authority with another (and often they contradict), by checking collateral evidence from Jewish, Greek, and Roman sources. A former colleague of mine, one who because of his own early experiences thinks religion unscientific and childish, was obviously shocked when before Christmas I told him that I thought Jesus was not born in Bethlehem; yet just those who believe religion worthy of adult appreciation have done the scholarly work that has identified the Bethlehem narratives as poetic propaganda for Christian Messianism. The general conclusion about Jesus is that he was indeed a historic figure, but that the narratives about him include many such elements of spontaneously generated myth. Let the reader notice, for example, the transition from the subjective experiences that St. Mark records for Jesus at his baptism, through two different externalizings in St. Matthew and St. Luke, to a totally objective report by the Fourth Gospel. Similarly St. Mark's one 'young man' at the empty tomb becomes 'an angel' in St. Matthew, 'two men in shining apparel' in St. Luke, and the mathematically inevitable 'two angels' in St. John.

Akin to uncritical secular courses in the literature of the Bible are the numerous 'literary' lives of Jesus that eminent littérateurs have ventured, usually late in their careers when their reputations were established and their minds closed. Some of these authors have said flatly that they have chosen to ignore the findings of New Testament scholarship, while others apparently have not even known that Biblical scholarship exists. Such works as those of Papini, Middleton Murry, and Hall Caine should be shelved not in the 200, 'religion' section of a Dewey decimal library, but in the 800, 'literature' department. They are more or less engaging as works of fiction. Because they are hopelessly lacking in scholarly treatment of the source material, they are under no circumstances to be regarded as legitimate biographies of the historic Jesus.

Historical criticism applies not only to Biblical times, but also to the entire history of religion. Historians of the Christian Church sometimes have been prejudicial propagandists for the Church as a whole, sometimes for their own respective branches of it. In this they have not differed much from historians of war or politics; and if they have not been superior as to academic conscience, they scarcely have been worse. It still is the duty of the sober ecclesiastical historian to report that there is no contemporary documentary evidence that Luther at the Diet of Worms said *Hier stehe ich*, just as it is the obligation of the American historian to challenge some details of the Lincoln and Coolidge and Roosevelt myths. If in either case the multitude prefers to cling to its myths anyway, that is not to be charged against the historians who have tried to teach it better. (Better, that is, as to fact; we should not forget that often the myth is the best possible summing up of the impact of a personality.)

The history of theological ideas is one which the Christian historian may by no means ignore. One principal reason for 'intellectual' contempt of Christianity has been the intellectuals' innocent sharing of uninformed and mistaken notions of the original nature and intent of historic Christian doctrines. What appear as manifest irrationalities in the Christian layman's thinking, and lamentably sometimes in current Christian preaching, look altogether different when seen in terms of backgrounds in Jewish and Hellenistic thought, and of development during the centuries of Christian history. The Fathers of the Church may not be easy reading; but those who will do the reading will learn of the doctrine, that it makes much more sense when one follows it through with scholarly patience than when one looks, carelessly and from without, only at its inadequately presented endproduct. Again the Christian scholar is the person who is entitled to an opinion; and it is unscholarly in the last degree to reject his conclusions without examining the evidence upon which he has based them.

Not only as to literature and history, but also as to psychology, religion must be submitted to careful and objective enquiry. Here the religiously minded have done quite as much work as have the non-religious; and arguably superior work, since they have had more direct and thorough acquaintance with the relevant data. The assumption of religious scholarship in this area is that the human personality is indivisible, and that its mechanisms are the same to whatever changing and miscellaneous concerns they may be applied. Thus prayer seen theologically may be believed to issue in direct apprehension of God; but prayer seen psychologically is a union of intellectual and affective processes which are as susceptible of psychological analysis as is the comparable mélange of human ideas and impulses which is called 'love.'

'I don't want to take Psychology of Religion,' protested a student (not at Mills College). 'I might lose my religious experience.' My answer was the one which I believe the scholars in this field would give with one voice: 'If your religious experience is of the kind that can be destroyed by psychological analysis, the sooner you lose it the better.' We need to remember here that the object of scientific study is to determine facts and to understand relationships. The study of the psychology of religion will in itself neither undermine true faith nor directly reënforce it. Its business is simply to observe religious faith as a psychological phenomenon, and so the better to understand its working in us.

That this observation can be carried out without forcing a conclusion either positive or negative is sufficiently shown in the respectively negative and positive conclusions about religion which have been reached by Freud and Jung. I would comment, however, that neither the negative position of Vienna nor the positive one of Zurich has any valid basis in the analysis of the psychic processes, seen as processes, which as psychologists the leaders of these schools were obligated to study. It was by non-rational, non-scientific faith that Freud said 'no,' just as it was by an equal though opposite faith that Jung said 'yes.'

The essential point in all this, and the one which prevailing academic superstition so often completely misses, is that almost all the wealth of exact scholarship about religion has been produced by those who themselves had faith as well as knowledge. Anti-religion has come forward with a mass of pseudo-scholarship, as for example in the attempts of a few nineteenth-century 'rationalists' to deny the historicity of Jesus: attempts which today are totally discredited, not because they were irreligious but precisely because they were unscholarly. The really rigorous treatment of the evidence belongs to those who have thought the subject-matter important enough to justify the burning of their midnight current, and sometimes the holocaust of long-prevailing but now demonstrably mistaken judgments.

Perhaps it should be said explicitly that the general point of view here outlined is not that of a radical minority, but one which is taken for granted by reputable scholarship in religion throughout the world. It is axiomatic for such learned bodies as the Society of Biblical Literature and Exegesis, and for the journals which in religion are the equivalents of the publications of scholarship in all the sciences and humanities. It is standard in the approved theological seminaries of every major Protestant Church in the United States, and equally it characterizes theological learning in Protestant Europe. Increasingly it is reflected in the preaching and teaching of the Churches, though in this writer's judgment not nearly explicitly and vigorously enough. If it were made better known, perhaps more of the irreligious at last would begin to hear about it.

This is not to say that there is anything like absolute unanimity among scholars in religion, any more than there is in economics or in biochemistry. The battles that are fought in the learned societies are of the same kind here as they are in the Modern Language Association or the American Philosophical Association. Every major theological faculty includes upholders of special hypotheses which they themselves have worked out, or which they have adopted from others, and which are eagerly assailed by many of their colleagues. (It is reported that Dr. E. F.

Scott, of Union Theological Seminary in New York, once said, 'I only wish we could get the public to realize that we of the Union faculty love one another, and hate one another's opinions.')

There are, however, two points that need here to be recognized. One is that all this controversy goes on, and that it can go on only, within a general framework of axiom and methodology which is wholly comparable to the accepted scholarly frameworks of other disciplines. Biblical scholars will differ sharply as to whether Ezra ever lived, or whether the 'love of God' passages were written by Hosea, or whether II and III St. John belong to the evangelist or to the apocalyptist. Church historians will debate the status of Athanasius in the Nicene Council, or the precise attitude of Calvin toward Servetus, or the balance between ritualism and revivalism in the writings of John Wesley. The scholars can differ and debate profitably, however, because they are scholars and because they operate in the same categories and apply the same kinds of criteria. They cannot profitably debate these points with the unscholarly, whether believing or unbelieving.

The second consideration to be noted is that the holding of a particular view about the Bible, or about the history of doctrine as history, has no direct correlation with the personal faith of the scholar in those realms which are not subject to historical criticism. Thus for example many of the neo-orthodox, whose faith in Christian doctrine is what is called 'high,' meaning that it strongly stresses the supra-natural, are among the most negative in their judgments of the precise historicity of the Gospels. Here then is clearly illustrated the distinction which exists, and which always must be maintained, between the scientific examination of data which give us factual answers, and the personal adventure of faith where factual data give no answer at all.

Judaism perhaps has had better fortune than has Christianity at the point of popular recognition of religious and specifically

Biblical scholarship. Learned Rabbis in all the centuries have done remarkable critical work, and their findings have secured appreciably wider dissemination within Judaism than have those of Christian scholars within Christendom. This is particularly true in the United States, where frontier distrust of 'eddication' has made life hard for professors in every field, and where popular suspicion of learning has created propaganda alike against braintrusters in Washington and against seminary teachers when they preach in the churches. The Jews, on the other hand, mostly escaped the frontier era in America, and they brought here with them their European respect for the learning of their Rabbinic scholars.

It was an exciting experience for the present writer, and I think for the audience, when recently students in a state college hurled the same Biblical and theological questions at a Rabbi and at me, seated side by side on a table at the front of a big lecture room; and when they got from us, time after time, identical answers in the literary and historical fields. The striking thing, however, was that the Rabbi was shocked at the ignorance and naïveté which the students revealed; whereas I, having lived long among Christians, was merely sorry without being surprised.

Scholars of the Roman tradition are in a peculiar position here. Many of them know the evidence, and within certain limits discuss it freely. I have known no more rigorous treatment of archaeological data, for example, than that of the Dominicans of the *École Biblique* in Jerusalem, whose insistence on valid historical proof often brought up short a Protestant inclined to wish-thinking. Since, however, the Roman form of 'Modernism' was officially condemned by Pius X in 1907, it is not possible for any Roman Catholic in good standing publicly to voice acceptance of some of the conclusions reported above. Nor is the recent beatification of this particular Pope a hopeful augury for the development, and the usefulness, of strictly objective scholarship under the Roman aegis.

The contrast here between the Roman and the Protestant patterns brings us back again to the distinction between faith and fact. In his bull against 'Modernism' Pope Pius was asserting as matters of faith a body of historical details which belong to the area of fact, and therefore to the field of scientific scrutiny. In so doing he confused the issue for every Catholic, and for many outside the Roman Church. Similarly Fundamentalism, erecting alleged fact into faith, has heatedly repudiated much that scholarship has proved. (I say 'proved' with intent; for such conclusions as the composite authorship of the Pentateuch, and the borrowings from St. Mark by St. Matthew and St. Luke, are as surely proved as is any explanatory hypothesis that has survived stringent testing in the laboratory.)

The scholar in the field of religion does not deny faith. If himself he is a religious person he asserts his faith with absolute conviction. But as a scholar he must deal with facts factually, with evidence critically, and with hypotheses logically. This he has done, and at least as long and as earnestly as the astronomers have dealt with the facts of the sidereal universe, or the biologists with the facts of organic life. He has been misunderstood by many, even as were Galileo and Darwin in their labors. It is a worse injustice and indignity that he has been ignored by so many more.

Religion as an academic discipline yields nothing in rightful status, nothing in intellectual integrity, to any department in the catalogue. Its practitioners, however, are humble men, and they have made less noise about their achievements than they might have been justified in making. This chapter has been a small attempt to blow the trumpet for them. It is time for the academic world to listen, and to learn what has been going on.

SUPERSTITION NO. 5

*that people who use symbols
have to take them literally*

The really curious fact about symbols is that almost everyone takes his own symbols symbolically, while he tends to charge all other people with taking theirs literally. Here it is necessary to define at the outset. A symbol is a representation. The essential point is that a symbol is not the object which it is used to represent. Nor is it a reasonably exact facsimile thereof. As my small desk dictionary puts it (the unabridged is more elaborate and less clear), a symbol is 'not . . . a portrait.'

What throws us off, and tempts us to treat the symbols of others more literally than we do our own, is the fact that any symbol becomes such within a given culture pattern, and through developments which only those who live inside the pattern can know. We who are external to a particular culture see first, and often only, its outer manifestations. Lacking the interpretive context which the culture provides for its own members, we are likely then to treat these manifestations as things in themselves, without recognizing their culturally determined overtones.

Thus, for example, it is very difficult for most young Americans to understand that while George VI reigns in Britain, he does not rule over the British people. A king is a king, says the (culturally) born republican, and so of course a British subject must be subject to his King. It requires a considerable mental effort, therefore, for an American to learn what every Briton knows, that the British King is wholly subject to his subjects' will as it is expressed through the voice of their Parliament. The precise way of describing this phenomenon is to say that His Britannic Majesty, while scarcely at all a monarch, is very definitely a symbol.

A symbol of what? Here it becomes evident that the real meaning of the symbol is accessible only in direct ratio to the degree of one's involvement in the culture. 'The King is a symbol of the Empire,' many an older Briton will say. But what is the British Empire? It turns out that this too is a symbol: not only a number of dominions and colonies, shown in symbolic red upon the symbol known as a Mercator map, but also and much more truly of attitudes built up among the British people, in divers portions and in divers manners, at least since the days of Elizabeth and probably from those of Harry of Agincourt. Because attitudes have changed to some extent, and for some people, there has arisen in our time the new verbal symbol of 'the British Commonwealth of Nations'; and so this symbol is what the younger Briton, and particularly the younger colonial, believes his King to symbolize.

There are, moreover, widely varying degrees of sophistication in the understanding of symbols by their users. A Dorset villager and Mr. Churchill may be equally loyal to their King, may even have comparable emotions when 'God Save the King' is sung. They do not have at all the same intellectual estimate of kingship, because they have had totally dissimilar experiences of it. That is to say, not only the history of a culture, but also personal histories within the culture, will determine what its symbols mean from day to day and from man to man.

The same principles apply, because the same factors are at work, for every kind of symbol that we know and use. Symbols are all about us, and symbolism is involved in almost all we do and certainly in all we say. Words themselves are symbols, universal as a phenomenon but highly particular for each several people. The difference between one language and another is the difference between the symbols that two separated cultures have developed to represent specific objects and ideas. *Trapeza* and *mensa* and *tavola* and *mesa* and *Tafel* all mean 'table,' each in one of those codes of symbols which are respectively the Greek, Latin, Italian, Spanish, and German languages. Incidentally one will note that, even though our English 'table' stands opposite each of these terms in the appropriate bilingual ·dictionary, no two of the terms are quite identical. *Trapeza*, for example, signifies also a bank (financial, not geographical), and *mesa* what more laboredly we call a table-land.

Gestures are symbols too, and also not quite universal in their denotation. The nodding head means 'yes' for us, but 'no' (and quite as reasonably by any dispassionate test) for a number of other peoples. Travellers in Arab lands have to learn for each locality the special gesture that means 'No, I really don't want any more coffee'; for in Eastern politeness the oral *la,* 'no,' is assumed to be politely meaningless. Clothes likewise, while serving something of a practical purpose, also are variously symbolic of nationality, of social class, to some extent of age, and notably of the types of occasions for which they are worn. There scarcely is a compelling rationale for white tie and tails; but there is a very real social compulsion about them, and a real emotional involvement in them, among the Four Hundred if not among the Four Million. For many a high-school youngster the cigarette is not at all a satisfaction (indeed often it is quite the opposite), yet decisively it is a symbol, and an important one, of growing up into freedom from an older generation's dominance.

Symbols thus stand for meanings in our life, for meanings socially shared. As new meanings develop, new symbols arise; and they are not only socially shared, but also socially selected. It was inevitable that religion, whose concern is with meanings and values, should create its own symbols to represent the values and the meanings which it held and sought. It was inevitable, too, that various systems of religious faith, growing up in various cultures, should produce widely variant modes of symbolic expression. It was inevitable no less that variant personal histories within each of these systems should give rise to variant apprehensions of the specific meanings thought to be involved. The symbol thus serves to reflect general identity, but always it includes a large proportion of specific variety.

Ever and again the fear that the symbol and the value have become confused, or that they are in danger of confusion, has led to the rejecting of the symbol in the hope of preserving the value. This is why Judaism, convinced that the alien Canaanites actually worshipped the carved or molten images which they used in worship, denied its own people not only the religious use of images, but also the privilege of making any visual representation whatever of living beings. Yet symbolism persisted, and within Judaism (as later in Islam) the very denial of artistic representationalism produced remarkable elaborations in abstract design. There survived, too, the tables of the law, the seven-branched candlestick, and the six-pointed star of David, all of them permissible because not depicting organic life; and these remained central in the decoration of buildings, in the usages of worship, and most of all in the feelings of adherents of the Jewish faith.

While Christianity began within a Jewish matrix, it moved rapidly into the Greco-Roman world and soon became naturalized therein. A primitive Jewish Christian might have been sensitive about the fish, the likeness of a living creature, as a token of his Christian allegiance; but a Greek or a Roman knew of no such taboo, and the drawing of the fish, or its carving on a tomb, was for him quite unexceptionable. Here is an interesting case of extreme distance, and of a curiously circuitous route, between symbol and meaning. The form of the fish reflected the Greek word *ichthus*, and the word was used because its letters were the initials of *Iesous Christos theou* (*h*)*uios soter*, 'Jesus Christ, Son of God, Saviour.' Yet once this connection was made, and the symbol generally recognized among Christians, the meaning was conveyed immediately by the picture; and conveyed no doubt quite adequately to Latin-speaking Christians who could by no means have reproduced the original Greek acrostic. Nor, we may note in passing, is there any evidence that the fish symbol ever led to the development of ichthyolatry in Christian circles.

Images of the Christ, of the Blessed Virgin, and of the saints, being more nearly in the nature of direct portraiture, more readily tempted the simple to confuse the physical object with the adored being. It seems to have been not only idolatry, however, incipient or actual among the Christians, but also the hope of the Eastern Emperor Leo III to make peace with the image-hating Saracens, that brought about the iconoclastic controversy of the eighth century. The Eastern Church at last settled down to its well-known compromise of permitting flat religious pictures in the churches, but never statuary in the round.

Statues persisted in the West, and led to a new iconoclasm (this time clearly deriving from fear of literal idolatry) in the Reformation. Protestant usage, while by no means uniform, seems commonly to imitate the Orthodox practice of approving two-dimensional religious art while rejecting three-dimensional. A curious distinction appears in some churches, where picture windows are readily accepted, but not paintings on the walls whether directly applied or merely hung. All this would seem to argue that statues are a temptation to their own worshipping, and that opaque pictures possibly are dangerous, but that a translucent picture is fairly sure to remain a symbol only.

What actually it demonstrates, of course, is that symbolism, while inescapable, is very difficult to deal with. The danger of identification ever is present. When it becomes notably apparent, they whose first concern is with the value are likely to become antagonistic toward the offending symbol. There is also a very common disposition to hate the symbols of values or ideas which one has rejected in their own character: as witness the intrinsically inoffensive but politically despicable swastika a decade ago, or the classic case of the Admiral who recently attacked the use of red stars in Christmas decorations because of the name of the Red Army journal. The extremists among the Protestant reformers, hating Romanism and with it the historic symbols of the Roman faith, thought to abjure symbols completely; so that not only the statuary, the stained glass, the clerical vestments, the incense and the candles, but the altar and the very cross, were by Separatists and Quakers ruled out altogether.

Immediately, however, the Protestant groups began to create new symbols of their own. The Puritan church building with its centered pulpit attested a central emphasis upon instruction rather than on sacramental worship. The bareness of the Friends' meeting house was not less symbolic than the elaborate decoration of the Catholic cathedral, and the studied lack of program for the Quaker Meeting produced its own special kind of ritualism. Even ministerial garb, no longer reproducing late Roman or early mediaeval fashions, became stylized in black instead of colors, and in fairly recent times provided identification of the nonconformists in their being (along with a few Down East undertakers) the only surviving wearers of the Prince Albert coat. One notes, in this connection, that the standard official dress of male Christian Science readers is a reproduction of formal lay apparel at the time their Church was founded, just as the older clerical vestments are approximations of prevailing clothing patterns in the days when European Christianity was taking form.

These new manifestations among the Protestant groups make it evident that symbolism scarcely is to be escaped. At the same time, their history shows that the substitution of one set of symbols for another is no guarantee that a new literalism will not arise. The centered pulpit and the undecorated wall and even the 'ministerial' garb came by many to be regarded as values in themselves, not less dear to their upholders than had been altar and pictures and vestments to the members of the older tradition.

It is evident also that the literal view of symbols may be held alike by those who use them and those who reject them. The fault, however, is not in the symbols themselves, but in the literal mind which apprehends them literally therefore wrongly. It is not high sophistication, but a lack of sophistication, that supposes the symbol and the meaning to be identical. The literal believer and the literally-minded unbeliever err equally in their failure to recognize that there never is a one-for-one correlation between the symbol and what it symbolizes.

The too simple notion that the symbol and the reality are one and the same is the essence of idolatry, and that whether in pagan lands or in historic cathedrals or in modern Biblicist sects. The irreligious are wholly right in condemning such idolatry where it exists. Their philosophical error stands in their thinking that it has to exist, and their historical error in supposing that it has been a prevailing character of religious thought and expression. 'The letter kills,' and literalism about symbols always has been deadly. But there is no need to choose this way of death; and St. Paul goes on to remind us that 'the spirit makes alive.'

Such an escape from bondage to the letter may make even the letter itself more significant. Seen as literal narrative, the book of Jonah is biologically, geographically, and historically absurd. When the work is recognized as being rather a symbolic assertion of God's concern with all men, including even the hated Assyrians as typical of Israel's national foes, and an assertion correlatively of man's obligation to serve his God, the 'great fish' at last disgorges, not indeed the prophet, but the prophet's living message. Quite probably, too, this book is a conscious allegory, the sea-monster being identified with Babylon, Jonah with Judah, and the 'swallowing' with the captivity; and in this case the symbolism, seen as such, proclaims the same high faith in Israel's mission to the world as is set forth explicitly by the second Isaiah.

One of the Christian symbols which has occasioned special controversy between literal believers and literal disbelievers is that whose proper name is itself 'Symbol': the 'Old Roman Symbol,' more familiarly known to us as the 'Apostles' Creed.'

The Creed is to be understood neither as a report of factual episodes, nor as an exact portrait of final truth, but as an attempt to reflect the values and the meanings which were accepted and held important by those who called themselves 'Christian.' That is to say, it is to be recognized as a Symbol in the precise sense of the term. When we recite the Creed we are sharing with the early Churches of Western Europe in declaring our allegiance to the cardinal values of the historic Christian faith. Thus we are expressing at once our fellowship with the continuing Church throughout the centuries, and our concern for the values which the Church has sought to make real in life. The principle of interpretation always must be the symbolic one: not that the Creed is the faith, but that it seeks to represent the common faith.

Thus the difficult expressions in the Creed, which one literal mind swallows without comprehending, and at which another literal mind boggles hopelessly, yield up their richness of meaning only to those who search beyond the symbol to the value: and the value is altogether likely to turn out to be acceptable, and deeply meaningful, to those who never could regard the declarations as statements of eternal fact. 'Born of the Virgin Mary,' improbable biologically and lacking such documentation as would impress a competent historian, becomes richly significant as a Hellenistic attempt to describe the observed quality of Jesus' life. 'He descended into hell,' difficult as to chronology and unthinkable as to cosmology, reveals itself as a statement of Jesus' full experience of human suffering, and also of the timeless universality of the salvation that the Church believes to be found through the Christ. 'Rose again from the dead' asserts the inevitable persistence of Jesus' kind of living as his followers had known it, and 'He ascended into heaven' is their symbolic way of declaring his elevation to the right hand of God as it had occurred in their own hearts.

With or without reference to Rimbaud, symbolism is of the nature of poetry. We have little difficulty with it when we are told that it is poetry with which we are dealing. Such a Hebrew couplet as 'The mountains skipped like rams, and the little hills like lambs,' never was regarded as fact by the many naïve readers who thought the story of Jonah factual, nor has it been scoffed at by those who think to laugh the great fish to scorn. The hymnals similarly are full of symbols which no one mistakes for outward fact: not even those who regard as factual the Creed that is said in the same service in which the hymns are sung. Since religion's realm is that of value rather than of fact, religion in particular must rely on symbols to express its values; but religion in particular, therefore, must free its mode of expression from any imprisonment within the literal, factual realm.

It is to be admitted, and positively asserted, that neither external symbols nor essential values appeal identically or equally to every person. Cultural conditioning, as we have observed, results in almost infinite personal variation. Sometimes two who share the value may differ sharply as to their symbolic preferences: as for example two Christian theists, one a Congregationalist and one an Episcopalian, who can agree in their theological belief but not on the use of a credal formula for it. Sometimes, again, the symbol may prove equally usable to two who give to it by no means the same content, as is illustrated Sunday after Sunday in those who together receive the Holy Communion; and here the symbol of the Eucharist provides a means toward effective unity of heart among those who are far from being one in mind.

There are three levels of symbolic usage, then, with which we have to reckon. The literal level of idolatry, whether of images or of words, the irreligious and the truly religious unanimously and properly will reject. The second level, an equally literal fear of imagery and beauty and outward expression, is one where misunderstanding still promotes conflict. It is no doubt childish to fail to make adequate distinctions between the seen and the unseen, between immediate and ultimate, between fact and truth: in short, between symbol and reality. But if this be the attitude of a child, the consequent effort to reject all symbols, just because some childish people have used them childishly, surely is itself only a stage of intellectual adolescence.

The third level, and the only mature one, is that in which we have learned to use religious symbols as they should be used: to represent in visible form the values that are unseen, to reflect truths that literally are beyond expression, to remind us by hearing and sight and action of the ideals we have chosen and by which we intend to live. In such maturity of approach, all the treasures of external beauty and of creative imagination are brought into the service of the true and the right. In the Church the Christian may see, if he will, the brightness of hope through the glad colors of the consecrated place. He hymns his joy through the noble cadences of the music. He declares his faith through the word symbols which he shares with those who in all these long centuries have engaged in the Christian quest for truth. He expresses his personal devotion to God through the restricted but meaningful gestures of standing to praise and kneeling to pray.

Of course we can be glad without color and song. We can set forth our faith in innumerable, ponderous volumes of prose instead of in a single soaring paragraph. We can be devout while sitting down, as countless American Protestants undoubtedly are. For many of us, however, the historic outward means of expression are a positive help toward our inward and spiritual grace. The ultimate goal must be in the realm of truth and value. The useful aid may be the symbolism of what in this sensory world we see and hear, of what we say and do.

The symbol of the cross provides the classic illustration. To suppose that we cannot worship without a cross, or a crucifix, is certainly infantile. To conclude that therefore we must never worship with one scarcely is grown up. Into a Methodist Church in Western Massachusetts, some thirty years ago, stepped a Portuguese workman. He looked around; and then, 'This ain't no Church,' he said; 'you ain't got no cross.' If we do not have the cross of Christ in our hearts, we are not members of any true Church of Christ. If we do have his cross on our altar, we may be reminded thereby both that he gave himself for man, and that by accepting the cross we also may live as he lives.

The poetry of a churchman has set forth the symbol and the meaning in one. Wrote John Donne, Dean of St. Paul's in London in a day when earnest reformers thought that to save the faith they must repudiate its every outward sign:

> Since Christ embraced the Cross itself, dare I
> His image, th' image of His Cross, deny?
> Would I have profit by the sacrifice,
> And dare the chosen Altar to despise?
> It bore all other sins, but is it fit
> That it should bear the sin of scorning it? . . .
> From me no pulpit, nor misgrounded law,
> Nor scandal taken, shall this Cross withdraw.
> It shall not, nor it cannot; for the loss
> Of this Cross were to me another Cross.

The cross indeed was a scandal, a stumbling-block, to many who heard of it in the first Christian century. Its physical representation has scandalized many since. Yet the rejection of the form, so far from preserving the essence, may contribute to the losing of the essence too. The cross and the altar recently have returned to many a Protestant church. It is at least possible that this will aid toward their return to some of our Protestant hearts.

The summary as to symbolism, then, is that superstition inheres always in literalness. Rightly the professed sceptic condemns the superstition of him who is literal in his using of the symbols. No less rightly may the religious person assail the superstition of him who is as crassly literal in his rejection.

We all use symbols, and in every area of our living, for we can do no other. We shall choose our symbols as our total cultural and personal settings will determine: settings which include such discussions of the problem and the details as we may share in. The crucial need is that we shall apprehend the values. If we are adult, and if we have any poetry in us, we shall recognize the symbols as instruments toward our apprehension.

SUPERSTITION NO. 6

that religion is an escape mechanism

⊂⊇ Under the laws of the State of California, a person indicted for murder may enter the dual pleas of 'not guilty' and 'not guilty by reason of insanity.' This is an extreme illustration of a common human response to accusation. Often when taxed with wrongdoing we say not either, but both, 'I didn't do it' and 'I did it because . . .'

Already it has become evident that this situation exists with reference to several of the charges commonly made against religion. In part they are not true; and in part, being true, they may be both understandable and defensible. The conservatism of religion is to some extent to be defended, since religion seeks to preserve historic values; yet at the same time religion often is seen to be not conservative at all, but vigorously revolutionary. Some religious men and movements have flown inexcusably in the face of fact and reason; but this is rigidly to be distinguished from religion's inherent and necessary quest beyond the realm of demonstrable knowledge. Symbols, instead of being servants of truth and value, sometimes by literalism have become overlords of thought and feeling; nevertheless symbols are not to be excised from life, and when rightly held they render useful service to us all.

The same duality, which need not be at all a dichotomy, exists as to the question of religion as an escape mechanism. To some extent religion has been an escape of timidity, of personal in-adequacy, of neurosis. To some extent it has been a legitimate means of controlling fear and failure and personal breakdown. This, too, may be called 'escape'; but only in the sense that es-cape from bondage is the way to freedom. To some extent, finally, and many will say to the largest extent, religion so far from being an escape has been sternly realist in its dealing with life, and for life has supplied a vital and positive challenge.

Let us deal with the concession first, and emphasize it. The consolations of religion sometimes have been sentimental, now and then altogether cowardly. Conversion on a raft in mid-Pa-cific lends itself readily to Freudian interpretation as sheer in-fantilism; and theistic belief spontaneously generated in the fox-holes does not commend itself as reflecting self-reliance either moral or intellectual. In less dramatic form the plea for religious escape is heard regularly by every parish minister in the pro-test, 'I don't want to be disturbed by the sermon when I come to church. I come to church to feel better.'

There is nothing new about this phenomenon, and nothing peculiar to Christianity. The world always has been too much with us, and most of the time too much for us. Man's wonder at the world, so often identified as the primal spring of religious feeling and thought, included not only his gladness in good weather but his unhappiness in bad, not only his gratitude for the grain but also his distaste for hail and drought. Political and social deprivation, too, sought compensations in a supra-hu-man world, and encouraged a flight from grinding present reality on the part of many oppressed, despairing persons and peoples.

Perhaps the charge most effectively to be pressed against his-toric religion, in this matter of escapism, is that of its having permitted, and even encouraged, flight from intellectual effort. The authoritarian Church falls readily under this condemna-tion, in so far as it presumes to relieve its adherents of the re-sponsibility of thinking for themselves. Manifestly many con-

verts to Rome have been driven chiefly by their increasing despair and their own intellectual confusions, as correlatively
they have been attracted by a Church which has worked out all
the answers and presents them as finished products.

Protestantism is by no means guiltless at this point. An authoritarian view of the Bible also provides escape from the obligation to think: at least so long as the individual does not hear too
many differing authoritative interpretations of the authoritative Bible's meaning. Even among the so-called 'liberals,' respect
for a clergyman's scholarship and sanity may lead to altogether
too ready an acceptance of his views, without any more critical
thinking than is engaged in by the lay Catholic. (I have learned,
for example, to distrust the mental processes of a student who
says too quickly that my attempted reply to a theological question
is altogether satisfying.)

While religion thus has convicted itself of allowing mental
slackness to the point of intellectual escape, it stands by no
means alone before this judgment. Several years ago, after hearing James Stephens speak at the University of California, I walked
away with a group of students. 'What an escapist!' said Jim, a
typical campus left-winger. After he had turned off on a side
path, one of the others remarked, 'Did it ever occur to you that
Jim is an escapist too?' And of course he was. He needed a fairy-
tale Russia just as Stephens needed a fairy-tale Ireland; and no
doubt both he and Stephens found in their respective fairylands
many of the same compensations that others have known in
Churches more generally recognized as such. The difference between the two was in Stephens' favor, for he knew his fairyland
to be one.

I pause to emphasize the intellectual escapism of some leftists I
have known. They are required by their dogma to scorn religion;
yet psychologically they are identical with the most abject non-
thinkers that ecclesiasticism and Biblicism ever have produced.
'What do you think of such-and-such an issue?' I asked a Communist who is by formal academic standards an educated man. 'I don't

know yet,' he said. 'The party line on that hasn't come out.' This differs not at all from the lay Catholic's reply, 'I can't answer that, but I know my priest can.' And so human nature, rather than religion, seems to be the principal source of trouble here.

Then there is the flight into religion from personal psychic strain. An elderly and witty Deaconess commented upon the general view that 'Deaconesses are women who have been disappointed in love.' There is just enough truth in that generally, though I assume not specifically with this Deaconess, to be disturbing. Factors of the same sort often are behind 'Get thee to a nunnery.' We should note, however, that both the Protestant and the Roman Churches have learned to be very careful about accepting neurotics into any special religious service, and that both insist on evidence of a positive vocation, rather than of merely negative flight, before granting admission.

Without joining religious orders, or entering upon professional religious activity, many have used religion as a curtain to shut off the unpleasant realities of their lives. Again the institutions of religion sometimes have been at fault here. Even like the cinema industry, they are tempted to give people what they think they want. Accordingly the love of Jesus is posed against the unfriendliness of the world, or the gifts of the Spirit against manifest deprivations of the body, or recourse to prayer as a substitute for personal effort, or (and all too often in Protestantism) the personal gentleness and warmth of the pastor as a surrogate for adequate adjustment to the community.

In its extreme form, this finding of outlets in religious emotion may dull even the moral sense. The excitements of the revival meeting have not always issued in sobriety or sexual self-discipline, and probably even less often in serious industriousness at work. The sect of the Khlysti in Czarist Russia frankly promulgated the doctrine of sin as the way to salvation, through the great joy to be found in human repentance and divine forgiveness: as a scathing line of D. H. Lawrence puts it, 'Sin your way to Jesus.' When the irreligious find fault with phenomena of this sort, most of the thoughtfully religious will agree with them.

Yet what is to be done about personal inadequacy in the face of overwhelming external confusions, an inadequacy which anyone but the most arrogant of self-worshippers finds recurringly in himself? Intellectual dictation from outside is obviously no answer, but intellectual stimulation may answer much. Sentimentality is no valid way out, but sublimation is approved by many who take psychology seriously though religion lightly. Emotional substitutes for action often are damaging to the human spirit; but emotion is precisely the motivating power needed to produce constructive action. Escapism we have so defined that it is by its definition unworthy: yet freedom of spirit everyone professes to want for himself, and to approve for others.

The claim of religion is that it does offer freedom, and can provide it: freedom 'from faithless fears and worldly anxieties,' freedom from self-pity, freedom from dependence on hope as a motive or success as a criterion. Schleiermacher did define religion as 'the sense of infinite dependence'; but another German theologian quickly pointed out that this would make the dog clearly more religious than his master. It is not the external prop, in this visible world or in a world unseen, that religion rightly offers man. It is precisely inward stamina.

That stamina becomes available to man as he lays hold on values which perdure beyond his daily circumstance, and as he commits himself wholly to those values as the end and the means of his living. If his values include God, as for the Christian they do, he believes that the presence of God may be actively powerful in his own life; and many a Christian will bear witness that this has happened, and does happen, in his experience. It is, however, a power to endure hardship, not a way to avoid it, that authentic Christianity holds God to give. Escape from suffering is not promised to them who would follow the Christ. What is promised is victory over suffering, in the conviction that the moment's personal affliction weighs but little in the scale of everlasting values.

Christianity, therefore, along with its parent Judaism, has been realistic from the beginning; and about the darker sides of life as well as the bright ones. With characteristic inconsistency those who blame the Christian Church for offering psychic escape, damn it at the same time for producing a 'guilt complex' by its emphasis upon the sinfulness of man. St. Paul and St. John never heard of complexes, but they were realistic practical psychologists, and they knew how fallible they and all men were. They knew, too, that their fallibility, and all men's, threatened the survival of any good in them or in their world. 'O wretched man that I am!' cries the apostle to the Gentiles; 'who shall deliver me from the body of this death?' 'If we say that we have no sin,' warns the Ephesian interpreter, 'we deceive ourselves, and the truth is not in us.'

Whatever may be the future of current neo-orthodoxy, it has made a mark that will not be erased, and should not be, in its stern recognition of the sinfulness of sin. This is not a discovery of the neo-orthodox, but a restatement of ancient and authentic doctrine. The easy escapes of self-justification, the facile rationalizations that make 'evil' no more than an anagram of 'live,' the light-hearted notion that to forgive is God's chief occupation: all these are repudiated not only by the neo-orthodox but also by the united voice of Judaism and Christianity from the primitive story of the expulsion from Eden to these dark days in which we live. Sin and evil are real. The religious man denies not their existence, but their right to triumph over him.

Moral escapism in the rejection of the category of sin appears most commonly not among Christians, but precisely among the irreligious who think to escape moral obligation by repudiating all moral standards. Some of these elaborately intellectualize their amorality, by turning the libido into an infallible if Unholy Ghost. Others, more casual, simply take the line of least resistance; and if they do not wind up in the divorce court or the penitentiary, it is by their good fortune rather than by their desert. (I will agree with them in refusing to credit their escape from serious penalty to any intervention on the part of God. All that needs to be said to them here is to remind them that God's mills grind slowly; and that is scarcely escapist doctrine.)

Along with the charge that Christianity says too much about sin is one to the effect that it is overmuch preoccupied with death. Here, too, the criticism is not one of escapism, but one centered on the historic Christian unwillingness to dodge basic issues. Yes, Christianity does have much to say about death; for it knows that, though death comes to all men and women, most of them do all they can to forget this final reality of earthly life, and they need to be reminded.

Memento mori in the nature of the case stirs no popular enthusiasm. To the contrary, popular parlance seeks to avoid the issue by using the circumlocutions 'passed away,' 'passed on,' 'left us,' or 'was taken,' instead of the direct, honest, and upsetting 'died.' Popular usage too, for which the sentimental clients rather than the imaginative undertakers ought chiefly to bear the blame, seeks to disguise the fact of death with 'slumber rooms' and 'columbaria,' with make-up on the corpse and flowers (or even, save the mark! canaries) in the chapel, and with the most saccharine of melodies on the organ. These palpable dishonesties are not religious, but purely secular; and if they are deemed cowardly and escapist, which they are, then the charge of escapism here lies against our American secular world rather than against religion.

The religious man then is thoroughly realist, not escapist at all. He sees life's horrors, and he confesses life's sin. He shares life's sorrows, he suffers life's pain, he moves on through life to certain death. He does not pretend that these are illusions, and he does not expect to find any way of passing them by. But he does not dwell on horror for horror's sake, nor does he journey to death in any morbidity of spirit. His attention, still and always, is on values, and his consecration is to the values in which as a religious person he believes.

Here the charge of escapism breaks down flatly and finally. Its very making, in the light of the history of religious leadership and religious loyalty, is evidence of the deepest historical ignorance. So far from escaping the unpleasant realities of life, or thinking to make light of them, the religious man by his very devotion may bring upon himself greatly increased suffering, and though not a more certain death certainly an earlier and more painful one.

Whether or not Abraham and Moses and Daniel ever lived, whether or not they did what the Old Testament narratives attribute to them, the very existence of the narratives attests the valuation which Judaism placed upon personal daring and persistent loyalty as expressions of the religious ideal. Among figures and events more certainly historical, the fearless assaults of Amos and Hosea and Micah, of Isaiah and Jeremiah, upon the *status quo* in ancient Israel and Judah, mark them as anything but escapist dreamers. They proposed positive programs in this world, in their own nations in their own time; and for their chosen values they dared all the contumely that an escapist majority lavished upon them in its anger at being asked to face the realities of its own being.

One hesitates even to mention the issue in the case of Jesus. The lives of the Hebrew prophets may be generally unfamiliar, but at least in outline that of Jesus is a matter of common knowledge. How anyone can seriously maintain that there was any escapism either in Jesus' message or in his life simply passes comprehension. The story of the temptation in the wilderness, at the very beginning of his active career, suggests three kinds of escape he might have chosen: that of material comfort, that of sensational popular success, that of compromise with things as they were. For moral reasons, for deeply religious reasons, Jesus rejected each of these escapes in turn. And so, even as Lent leads to Good Friday, those first decisions in the desert pointed the way straight to the cross.

Nor does the history of Jesus' followers give any support to the proposition that it was an escapist gospel they had thought to find in him. St. Paul may annoy us a bit by his conscious and assertive sense of martyrdom, but there can be little doubt that the catalogue of hardships he wrote out in bitter self-defensive argument with his Corinthian critics is reasonably exact:

In labours more abundant, in stripes above measure, in prisons more frequent, in deaths oft. Of the Jews five times received I forty stripes save one. Thrice was I beaten with rods, once was I stoned, thrice I suffered shipwreck, a night and a day I have been in the deep; in journeyings often, in perils of waters, in perils of robbers, in perils by mine own countrymen, in perils by the heathen, in perils in the city, in perils in the wilderness, in perils in the sea, in perils among false brethren; in weariness and painfulness, in watchings often, in hunger and thirst, in fastings often, in cold and nakedness. Beside those things that are without, that which cometh upon me daily, the care of all the churches.

A cleric cannot resist the comment that the care of the churches no doubt was the gravest hardship of them all; and his brethren of the cloth will certify that there is no escape from the reality of life in the work of any parish.

Ultimately St. Paul ended his career as a prisoner in Rome, and almost certainly he met his death in the persecution under Nero. Christianity had proved to be no easy thing, had provided no escape mechanisms, for this greatest of its apostles. The space would fail us to call the roll of those who suffered after him, but with him in loyalty and in full freedom of choice. The noble army of martyrs gained many recruits through the years before Constantine, and it did not fail of enlistments thereafter. A youngster born in China just before the turn of the century cannot forget the simple Chinese, as well as the missionaries, who died during the Boxer rising rather than recant. They may have been misguided, they may have been fools as the world knows wisdom; but none can count them escapist.

There remains one stock answer yet. It is that the escapism of Christianity inheres in its otherworldliness, so that even voluntary martyrdom may be escapist in essence, because it is flight from present problems into the promise of an eternally blessed future. Bernard Shaw did an excellent job of handling this in *Androcles and the Lion*, where the man with the martyr complex loses both this life and that to come, while the simple, practical Christian manages without forethought to preserve himself now, and still to retain a fair chance for the hereafter. It would not have surprised Mr. Shaw, who was a better theologian than often is recognized, to be told that the authentic voice of the Church is with him and with his humble Androcles.

The difficult Calvinist doctrine of foreordination here expresses the fundamental principle as Christianity sees it. Promises of reward in the hereafter have been made in the Church, as indeed they seem now and then to be made in the Scriptures; but the promises never are absolute, whereas the requirements definitely and uniformly are. Listen to Jesus as he leads the way on that last solemn journey to Jerusalem, where he knows as surely as one may know cause and effect that death awaits him:

> Ye shall indeed drink of the cup that I drink of: and with the baptism that I am baptized withal shall ye be baptized: But to sit on my right hand and on my left hand is not mine to give: but it shall be given to them for whom it is prepared.

Again it is to be noted, as with the early Hebrew stories, that the presence of this saying in the accepted Scriptures indicates the authentic view of the Church which gave the Scriptures circulation. That view, here set forth with unmistakable clarity, is specifically that the claims of the Christian life carry with them no assurance of pleasant recompense, either before death or after it.

The simple statement of the case in St. Mark's Gospel is completely at one with the profound philosophical insight of the writers of the symposium which is the core of the book of Job. (The reader is reminded that he should disregard the last chapter of that work, which is addendum and sheer heresy; and escapist if one wishes to call it that.) A certain type of Jewish thought, quite possibly shared by a popular majority though not for that reason to be esteemed as orthodox, had accepted a commercialized, *quid pro quo*, doctrine of the relationship between righteousness and reward. This was conceived to be worked out unfailingly in this world, and is expressed in its classic form in the Psalm verse, 'I have been young, and now am old; yet have I not seen the righteous forsaken, nor his seed begging bread.'

The authors of the Job symposium had observed that this simply was not true in their experience, and they wrote their argument in the form of a case study of a righteous man who was forsaken indeed. Later misreadings and mistranslations have seemed to introduce a couple of suggestions of reward in a future life, but critical readings of the text support the general implication of the debate. That is simply that there is no sort of escape contemplated for Job except the silence of death, and no possible reward except his consciousness of his own rectitude. Thus the authentic text of the work culminates in the tremendous oath of clearance in the thirty-first chapter:

> If my land cry against me, or that the furrows likewise thereof complain; If I have eaten the fruits thereof without money, or have caused the owners thereof to lose their life: Let thistles grow instead of wheat, and cockle instead of barley. The words of Job are ended.

A cognate witness from yet another culture is the *Bhagavadgita*. I happened a few months ago to mention to a young Hindu that I found much of spiritual guidance and strength in the *Gita*. Immediately he quoted the lines which have meant to me most of all:

> Thy business is with deeds alone,
> Not with the fruits the deeds may yield.

The whole argument of the *Gita* is that man must do his duty, without concern for result. The divine charioteer, the Lord Krishna, examines the ways of the religious life: the way of knowledge, the way of devotion, the way of action. But all of them point to this one absolute principle, that man's concern is to fulfill himself in loyalty to the obligations that he has accepted. There is no assurance of success, none of personal reward. There is merely duty to be done.

This is the voice of religion rightly understood, and this is the final answer to the escapist charge. The real escapists are they who flee from duty, whether their flight be into fantasy, or into liquor and sex, or merely into laziness. The actual cowards in this world are they who will not seek values worth living for and dying for. And these escapists, these cowards, are not they whom the challenge of religion has captured for its own.

SUPERSTITION NO. 7

that religious people are socially unconscious

◖◗ In these days of ever-heightening social tension, of recurring social crisis, the charge that religion is socially useless, or worse, is made in many circles. The extreme form of the allegation is the Marxist one, which represents religion as a deliberate conspiracy for the repression of the masses of mankind, and against their material wellbeing. Akin to this, and no more complimentary even though less angry, is the common assumption, among intellectuals who are proud of their own 'social consciousness,' that religion is a middle-class hideout, wholly irrelevant to the struggles of man, entirely shut off from the realities of human need and conflict. The two views are very closely similar, the one being in essence that religion is a negative force in the social scene, the other that it is a nonentity. A positive reply therefore may be attempted, as to most points, to the two criticisms at the same time.

The casual quoting of Marx about religion as 'the people's opiate' seldom gets down to specific reference, or to thought of context either verbal or historical. This once let us hear Mr. Marx speaking for himself, in the critique of Hegelianism (*Zur Kritik der Hegelschen Rechtsphilosophie*) first published in 1843:

> Man makes religion; religion does not make man. Religion, indeed, is the self-consciousness and the self-feeling of the man who either

has not yet found himself, or else (having found himself) has lost himself once more. But man is not an abstract being, squatting down somewhere outside the world. Man is the world of men, the State, society. This State, this society, produce religion, produce a perverted world consciousness, because they are a perverted world. . . .

Religion is the sigh of the oppressed creature, the feelings of a heartless world, just as it is the spirit of unspiritual conditions. It is the opium of the people. The people cannot be really happy until it has been deprived of illusory happiness by the abolition of religion. The demand that the people should shake itself free of illusion as to its own condition is the demand that it should abandon a condition which needs illusion.

This is unquestionably able writing, and palpably sincere; and it is not surprising that liberals as well as Marxists have been greatly impressed by it (or, perhaps more commonly, by its echoes). If the case can be proved as set forth in the indictment, the religious person is not only the spokesman for illusory happiness, for personal escapism, but also for a deliberate and quasi-official determination to hold the 'oppressed creature' firmly bound in his social captivity, and for a 'perverted world' which has no intent to give up its perversions. Conviction of religion on this charge rightly should issue in sentence of exile if not of death.

The question is whether the charge can be sustained. What evidence supports it, in the world of Marx and in history before and after him? What evidence, if any, is to be adduced to the contrary?

The religion which Marx knew at firsthand was official, formal religion in the Rhineland in the first half of the nineteenth century. By ancestry a Jew, Marx resented not only the humiliation of the Jews in the continental European scene, but also, and furiously, his own Jewishness. They who applaud the Communists for their freedom from racism, the while they share the Communist reverence for Marx's writings as a new and greater Holy Writ, will do well to read his bitter essay on 'The Emancipation of the Jew.'

'What was the foundation of the Jewish religion?' he asks; and he replies:

> Practical needs, self-interest. . . . Money is the jealous God of Israel, by the side of which no other god may exist. . . . What remains as the abstract part of the Jewish religion, contempt for theory, for art, for history, for man as an end in himself, is the real conscious standpoint and virtue of the monied man.

And he expresses his confidence that society at last will abolish 'the empirical essence of Judaism, the huckster.'

Yet in all this, and throughout the essay, it is evident that actually it is not the Jewish faith, not its theory nor its history, but rather the life of the bourgeois, non-religious Jews of the German principalities, that has stirred the revolutionary fury of the man who was born into their milieu. Never does Marx discuss the Judaism of the Scriptures, of the Talmud, of the Rabbis. His eyes are only on his contemporary scene, and they are fixed on that part of it which has departed furthest from the essential Jewish tradition.

Karl Marx was baptized as a Protestant when he was six years old. There is no sign that his father's decision to embrace Christianity arose from any profound change of religious conviction; and it is certain that the son shows no more surviving deposit of Christian training than he does of Jewish erudition. It seems fully reasonable to assume that the 'conversion' of the Marx family was a conversion of convenience, one of the kind that numerous non-religious Jews underwent in order to escape the social and political stigmata of their Judaism. Thus it was a change from one essentially non-religious formula to another, without concern for intellectual content and without any vestige of appreciation of spiritual values.

That there were genuine spiritual values in the German Protestantism of the time is undeniable. It is also true, however, that from Martin Luther's day onward the Germans among all Protestants had concerned themselves least with the relevance of religion to the social experience of man. Though the Lutheran

Church was a state Church, its explicit position was that the state should deal with all material and 'practical' concerns, and that the decisions of the state were to be subjected neither to ecclesiastical nor to religious review. By its silence thus the Church gave its consent to all that the state might see fit to do; and since the state was concerned to maintain the *status quo*, the Church became a silent partner in this maintenance.

In this period, too, the social relevance of the Catholic faith was at one of its least visible points in history. The Church long had been involved in the political strife of the upper echelons, and it found itself now in close alliance with the monarchism that already was fighting a rearguard action on the West European field of battle. True, the mass of the Catholic laity, and indeed of the clergy, were simple believers. But they were perhaps a shade too simple to understand fully what was happening. Since the French revolution had been so aggressively atheist, it seemed obvious that a Catholic ought to be counter-revolutionary. Compensations and consolations were found, even as Marx declared, in the realm of miracle in this life and in the hope of eternal rest and perpetual light in the life to come.

Thus what Marx had seen of religion, in his own immediate environment, lent itself readily enough to his interpretation; and this sort of religion, without reference to possible 'mitigating circumstances,' may seem to have merited his sentence of annihilation. The difficulty here is that which is evident elsewhere in Marx's writing: namely, that he selects his evidence from an extremely narrowed field, and calmly ignores any datum which might support a different conclusion. Notice, for example, the outright limitation in his preface to the first edition of *Das Kapital:*

> In this work I have to examine the capitalist mode of production, and the conditions of production and exchange corresponding to that mode. Up to the present time, their classic ground is England. That is the reason why England is used as the chief illustration of my theoretical ideas.

Those theoretical ideas, however, were promptly applied to the entire world scene; with the interesting result that in Lenin's day, since Russia had no industrial proletariat to illustrate the doctrine, it seemed to the Bolsheviks necessary to create one. Just so, the classic ground of socially irrelevant religion was for Marx the series of manifestations he had seen in the Rhineland as a child and as a young man. (He saw no manifestations after, being immured permanently in the reading room of the British Museum.) Therefore he used this formal religion, of one small region in one half-century, not only as 'the chief illustration of [his] theoretical ideas' about religion, but also as their total basis. The longer histories of Judaism, Roman Catholicism, and Protestantism, their past services to mankind and their social potentialities, he totally ignored as indeed he was wholly ignorant of them.

Yet it is with history that we are dealing, and it is only by the long-range witness of history that the dictum of the religious opiate may fairly be tested. Has religion been indeed an opium commonly given to the people to keep their senses dulled? Has it, in alliance with things as they are, resisted the human world that ought to be? As in the other areas we have considered hitherto, so here we must give heed not alone to popular frailties, but also and primarily to the authentic voice of leadership. Religion at its worst, and perhaps in its majority expressions, admittedly has been guilty of social unawareness and sometimes of social criminality. Religion at its best has spoken and done otherwise; and he who defends religion is entitled to contend for religion at its best: to contend for it in argument, as ever he must contend for its realization in life.

Perhaps Marx did not know it, and in any event he never would have admitted it, but his own social concern was rooted authentically and deeply in the prophetic passion of his own Hebrew heritage. The very founder of the Israelite religious system was by the approved tradition reported to have been no willing conformist, and no encourager of conformity on the part of others. Moses might have lived a quite unexciting and useless, but very comfortable, life in the palace of the Pharaoh. Instead, the record clearly says, Moses led a great strike in the building trades down by the Nile, and followed that up by directing one of the great mass migrations of all history. Nor is there any hint that he ever supposed he might fulfill his social responsibility by withdrawing to Babylonia and holing up there to produce learned treatises in the library of Hammurabi.

On more certain historical ground, we should note the essential democracy, and the critical need of communal responsibility, in the life of the wandering tribes in the desert. Life for them was not easy, and survival always was managed by the narrowest of margins. Since there was no economic surplus, there was no room for inequity. Since there was constant danger, there must be continuing unity. The tribes symbolized all this in the communion meal, the earliest and most meaningful of religious sacrifices: and this has survived in the Jewish Passover and in the Christian Eucharist. Equally, and more significantly as to what troubled Mr. Marx, the desert tradition of human brotherhood always was a critical point of reference for the teaching, and the spirit, of the later Hebrew prophets.

The settlement in Canaan involved the building of a nation, and so revolutionism (except for developing palace squabbles) long was beside the point. One may note in passing that the condemnation at Ai of Achan's whole family, which to us seems so brutal, reflects from the Israelite point of view the conviction that the gain of one had to become the benefit of all, and so that they who profited selfishly at the expense of the community must be wiped out. As the years passed, and Israel became a successful agricultural people, the old unities broke apart. There now were stronger and weaker, richer and poorer; and so it was time for revolutionary religion to assert itself.

It did so in the desert-born Amos, thundering out his God's condemnation of those who 'sold the righteous for silver, and the needy for a pair of shoes.' It did so in the small farmer Micah, calling down God's vengeance on them who 'covet fields, and take them by violence.' It rang out from the very mansions of the aristocracy as Isaiah, a traitor to his class if ever there was one, cried his

> Woe to them that join house to house, and field to field, till there be no place, that they may be placed alone in the midst of the earth.

It was declared in the very Temple gates, as Jeremiah demanded that his people should

> thoroughly amend your ways and your doings . . . thoroughly execute judgment between a man and his neighbour . . . oppress not the stranger, the fatherless, and the widow.

Not one of these men proffered opium to the downtrodden. Not one of them suggested that the poor and the helpless should be content with their lot. And these were they whom Israel regarded as the prophets of the Lord, whose writings the scribes preserved and recopied, and whose judgments became the nation's authority.

Did Lenin analyze and condemn brutal, grasping, arrogant imperialism? He may not have read the prophets; but if he had, he would have found agreement (and more eloquent statement than his own) in what they had to say of the empires of old. Isaiah saw at the end of the eighth century B.C. that the top-heavy structure of the Assyrian regime must fall of its own weight. Into Assyria's mouth he puts the authentic imperial boasting of any century, including our own:

> I have removed the bounds of the people, and have robbed their treasures. . . . My hand hath found as a nest the riches of the people: and as one gathereth eggs that are left, have I gathered all the earth; and there was none that moved the wing, or opened the mouth, or peeped.

But the contradictions of imperialism were deadly long before Lenin. Isaiah continues:

Therefore shall the Lord, the Lord of hosts, send among his fat ones leanness; and under his glory he shall kindle a burning like the burning of a fire . . . and it shall burn and devour his thorns and briers in one day; and shall consume the glory of his forest, and of his fruitful field. . . . And the rest of the trees of his forest shall be few, that a child may write them.

When Assyria had fallen, just as Isaiah had discerned that it must, Nahum sang an exulting paean that may not be 'Christian' in spirit but certainly is not collaborationist in attitude:

Thy crowned are as the locusts, and thy captains as the great grasshoppers, which camp in the hedges in the cold day, but when the sun ariseth they flee away, and their place is not known where they are. Thy shepherds slumber, O king of Assyria: thy nobles shall dwell in the dust: thy people is scattered upon the mountains, and no man gathereth them. There is no healing of thy bruise; thy wound is grievous: all that hear the bruit of thee shall clap the hands over thee: for upon whom hath not thy wickedness passed continually?

Probably it was of Alexander rather than of Nebuchadrezzar that Habakkuk wrote:

Because thou hast spoiled many nations, all the remnant of the people shall spoil thee; because of men's blood, and for the violence of the land, of the city, and of all that dwell therein.

Whether it was of Macedon or Babylon, however, it was of imperialism; and it was not in consent to rapacity, but in a burning sense of injustice, that this man of God, with his precursors, spoke of the self-generating vengeance that must fall on him who is inhumane to man. Perhaps there are reasons, after all, why the Soviet philosophers prefer not to read the Hebrew prophets in this latter day.

The early Christian leaders were less explicit about economics and politics than had been the prophets of the former times. This seems to have been due principally to two factors: first, that the power of Rome appeared so absolutely overwhelming as to permit no thought of possibly successful action against it, or even of effective criticism within it; second, that prevailing Jewish apocalyptic, itself a product of despair of direct political and social action, so affected the primitive Church that most of its people expected a supernatural and almost immediate ending of the existing world. Yet it is manifestly absurd to argue that early Christianity, whether seen in Jesus or in his followers, was wholly indifferent to the physical and social needs of man. The Teacher and the apostles dealt with man personally, and on the smaller scale of immediate acquaintance; but they dealt with every need of man's living on this earth.

The same Gospels which record Jesus' quoting of 'Man shall not live by bread alone' tell of his concern that the hungry multitude shall be fed. If this episode, which partakes of the nature of miracle, be set aside as myth, it still represents what the reporters of it thought important. There remains also the Sermon on the Mount, with its 'Give to him that asketh thee, and from him that would borrow of thee turn thou not away,' and its 'Do good to them that hate you.' We recognize too the striking concern of the physician St. Luke with the deprived and the despised of the community, illustrated not only in the parables of the lost sheep, the lost son, and the lost coin, of the good Samaritan and of Dives and Lazarus, but also in the episodes of the Samaritan leper and of Zacchaeus the tax collector.

The New Testament writings other than the Gospels speak with a divided voice about the proper Christian attitude toward the *status quo* of the Mediterranean world. St. Paul and the author of I St. Peter seem to have no thought of accomplishing major social change, but they plead for fellowship among the faithful and for honesty and goodwill toward all. The letters known as Jude and II St. Peter, the latter borrowing much from the former, present in contrast a bitter indignation with the 'Sodom and Gomorrah' amid which the authors live. That their only solution is a cataclysmic one has obscured the pointed criticism which they make, and which in their humble situation was all they could contribute. The book of Revelation, too, expects

God to solve the world's problems by external intervention; but certainly it never suggests that the Christian should be at all content with things as they are under the Domitianic rule. Indeed, its elaborate symbolism is itself witness to the compelling necessity that the intent of such subversive literature should be carefully concealed from the Roman secret police.

Too little is generally known, again, and so too little recognition is given, as to the great and creative social services which Christian idealism rendered in the later history of Rome and of Europe. Slavery as a system remained a moot question, even St. Paul failing to make himself quite clear in his letter to Philemon; but the voluntary manumission of slaves became almost a standard symbol of Christian conversion among those who had owned them. The Church's forbidding of usury commonly is mentioned by economic historians only as the cause of the Jewish monopoly of money-lending; yet its motive as a safeguard against oppression and extortion surely ought to be noted in estimating what the Church thought to be relevant to Christian duty. The concept of a 'just price' also, however shaky as an economic proposition or unenforceable as a practical measure, attests the fundamental concern of official Christianity with fundamental justice among men.

It was St. Thomas who said that 'a man should not look on external goods as private, but as common.' And this principle he followed through by declaring that 'The superabundant wealth of some is by nature due to the poor.' One surely hears in this an echo of the earlier and angrier Basil: 'It is the bread of the famished you hoard, the money of the needy that you keep buried.' The mediaeval synthesis was to a large extent static, and ultimately it had to give way to new forces. But all that was best in it, all that was humane and gentle and gracious, is to be credited to a Church which had not wholly forgotten the humaneness, the gentleness, the graciousness of its Lord.

Protestantism at first fell far below the historic Catholic

standard of social awareness. No honest and informed Protestant will pretend that the first great reformers were evangelists of the social gospel. As children of the Renaissance they were individualists to begin with, and their rebellion was inescapably an individual one. Becoming then involved in politics, Luther in Germany and Calvin in Geneva were driven by circumstance to defend social order without giving primary attention to social need. From Luther, who had to retain the support of the German princelings if either he or his movement were to survive, there stemmed the historic unwillingness of Lutheranism to concern itself with mundane affairs. From Calvinism, as Tawney has shown so compellingly, arose that 'triumph of the economic virtues' which has caused rugged individualism so often to be mistaken for Christian probity.

Yet it was not long until the original Christian witness to a basic social ethic reasserted itself in Protestant circles. The Quakers were among the first in point of time, as ever they have been in point of sincerity and of amazingly effective service. Fox proclaimed the cause of peace, Bellers pioneered the reform of the Poor Laws, Penn for a time made brotherly love real along the upper Delaware, and John Woolman assailed slavery long before that system showed itself to be impracticable, and therefore easily to be condemned, in the Northern colonies. It is worth remembering too, and especially by those who admire the activities of the National Maritime Union, that Woolman was one of the first to protest against the brutal conditions of life that the eighteenth century forced upon seamen.

The Wesleyan revival was devotional, and more churchly than most modern Methodists realize. Nevertheless it was driven forward also by intense concern for the wellbeing of the British common people, not only the rural villagers but also the miners and the newly developing class of the factory hands. He who was forbidden the pulpits preached at the pitheads; and, if Lecky be right, thereby saved Britain from the agonies of a Reign of Terror. This of course may be regarded by professional and amateur revolutionaries as a debit rather than a credit item in religion's account; but the general course of British history suggests that it is unimaginative sentiment rather than historical good sense that would substitute a Jacobin Mountain's procedures for Parliament's repealing of the Corn Laws.

The further development of capitalist industrialism posed ever new problems to those who, true to the essence of the Hebrew-Christian religion, could not hold it separate from life. As we come into modern times we see the spokesmen of Christianity one after another wrestling with the human chaos that ordered industry had created. It is fundamental dogma for Marxists that they should anathematize 'Christian Socialism.' Yet they should be reminded that F. D. Maurice used (some hold he originated, but this I doubt) the 'religion is opium' dictum: not indeed to condemn all religion indiscriminately, as had the less perceptive Marx, but strenuously to challenge the false religion of the landed aristocracy and the Manchester manufacturers. The founders of the Labour Party were in part the London intellectuals, some of them churchmen and some not, of the Fabian Society. They would have remained merely a debating club, however, had they not become allied with the British workmen of the trade unions; and many of the principal leaders of the unions had had their first experience of leadership, and of public speaking, as local preachers of the Wesleyan circuits.

The first notable pronouncement that bore official and general Christian authority came from the most authoritative Christian personage then living: His Holiness, Pope Leo XIII. In the *Rerum Novarum* of 1891 Leo took account of such 'new things' as corporate monopolies, factory labor, and trade-union organization. Noting from his point of view that some existing unions were antipathetic to religion, the Pope frankly called on Christian workmen to 'form associations among themselves—unite their forces and courageously shake off the yoke of an unjust and intolerable oppression.' That oppression he had defined unmistakably in an earlier section, and had taken sides squarely against it:

The first concern of all is to save the poor workers from the cruelty of grasping speculators, who use human beings as mere instruments for making money. It is neither justice nor humanity so to grind men down with excessive labor as to stupefy their minds and wear out their bodies.

Leo paid attention to such practical matters as the propriety of shorter hours for those who did the harder work, such as mining, and he advanced the then revolutionary idea that 'work which is suitable for a strong man cannot reasonably be required from a woman or a child.'

All this, let it be remembered, is the authoritative voice of him who was the Vicar of Christ for a major segment of Christendom. Much of the encyclical now sounds politically and socially naïve, and many of its suggestions are for today commonplace. They were neither so commonplace nor so naïve when they were written, and they set official Roman Christianity not among the laggards, but in the forefront, of the march toward social justice on the earth.

Forty years after, Pius XI in *Quadragesimo Anno* reëxamined Leo's statement, and rephrased the Catholic position in terms of what had happened since. One evening I read a long section of this encyclical to a well informed friend, and asked him to name the author. 'That's easy,' he said. 'Of course it's John Maynard Keynes.' It is possible that Pius may have borrowed from Keynes' earlier works, though since the encyclical was published in 1931 it scarcely can have been dependent on the Keynesian classic, *The General Theory of Employment, Interest and Money*, which did not appear until 1936. Whomever he may have been quoting, Pius still was uttering the voice of the Church, and of a religious point of view which no fair mind can think indifferent to the contemporary social and economic scene.

Quite flatly, to the contrary, the Pope declared that

though economic science and moral discipline are guided each by its own principles in its own sphere, it is false that the two orders are so distinct and alien that the former in no way depends on the latter.

With reference to economic control by a small financial oligarchy, he pointed out that

> It is patent that in our days not alone is wealth accumulated, but immense power and despotic economic domination is concentrated in the hands of a few, and that those few are frequently not the owners, but only the trustees and directors of invested funds, who administer them at their good pleasure.

> This power becomes particularly irresistible when exercised by those who, because they hold and control money, are able also to govern credit and determine its allotment, for that reason supplying so to speak, the life-blood to the entire economic body, and grasping, as it were, in their hands the very soul of production, so that no one dare breathe against their will.

> This accumulation of power, the characteristic note of the modern economic order, is a natural result of limitless free competition which permits the survival of those only who are the strongest, which often means those who fight most relentlessly, who pay least heed to the dictates of conscience.

Accordingly, the Pope held:

> Wealth . . . which is constantly being augmented by social and economic progress, must be so distributed amongst the various individuals and classes of society that the common good of all . . . be thereby promoted. . . . By these principles of social justice one class is forbidden to exclude the other from a share in the profits.

One more quotation, evidently a favorite of Pius since he himself reused it later in *Divini Redemptoris,* his most vigorous attack upon 'atheistic Communism,' will suffice to set forth the Christian economic position as this successor of St. Peter saw it:

> Then only will the economic and social order be soundly established and attain its ends, when it offers, to all and to each, all those goods which the wealth and resources of nature, technical science and the corporate organization of social affairs can give. These goods should be sufficient to supply all necessities and reasonable

comforts, and to uplift men to that higher standard of life which, provided it be used with prudence, is not only not a hindrance but is of singular help to virtue.

That is to say, His Holiness believed a higher standard of living in this world to be an aid toward Christian virtue. Who then can charge his Church with treating Christianity as irrelevant to a higher standard of living?

Among Protestants there were similar stirrings, in the nineteenth century with Maurice and Charles Kingsley in England and with the Church Association for the Advancement of the Interests of Labor here. That society was Episcopalian. A leading figure in molding the Christian social conscience was the Congregational minister, Washington Gladden. In 1903 a Department of Church and Labor was organized by the Northern Presbyterians. Perhaps the most decisive personal catalyst was a Baptist Professor of Church History (is not his field relevant?), Walter Rauschenbusch, whose *Christianity and the Social Crisis*, first published in 1907, is the Magna Charta of the 'social gospel' in America. The first Church to take a strong official position was the Methodist, with the 'Bill of Rights' which its General Conference adopted in 1908.

Thus the social relevance of Christianity was becoming recognized in all the major communions of American Protestantism. The Methodist 'Bill of Rights,' slightly rephrased but not at all toned down, became in that same year the first 'Social Creed of the Churches,' by action of the organizing convention of the Federal Council of Churches of Christ in America. Already at that date, when William Howard Taft was making a runaway race for the Presidency, the united voice of Protestantism in the United States declared for 'the right of employes and employers alike to organize,' for 'a living wage for all and the highest wage which each industry can afford,' for 'the most equitable division of the product of industry that can ultimately be devised.' In 1932, in the days of the deepest depression and before the dawning of the New Deal, the Federal Council revised its Social Creed to declare its support of 'social planning and control of the social and monetary systems and the economic processes for the common good,' and of 'social insurance against sickness, accident, want in old age, and unemployment.' Now do the non-religious Rooseveltians know why their hero remained a churchman? And can they guess where he may have picked up some of his ideas?

The United Steelworkers of America among all the CIO unions have most skillfully and most successfully guarded themselves from ever falling under Communist control. Their union therefore probably includes a negligible number of doctrinaire Marxists. Perhaps not all of the members active today, however, know how much their predecessors in the employ of the steel industry owed, and how much correspondingly they themselves owe, to the publication of a report on the steel strike of 1919 by a committee of the Inter-church World Movement headed by Bishop F. J. McConnell of the Methodist Episcopal Church. It is universally recognized, among those who know the story, that it was this report which so stirred up public opinion that management had to yield, and to institute an eight-hour day instead of the long maintained and stubbornly defended twelve-hour shift. Has any Communist front organization, or any coterie of 'liberals' assembled to drink cocktails and rail at fortune, accomplished half as much?

Even as the first convention of the Federal Council adopted the Social Creed, so also the organizing assembly of the World Council of Churches, held in Amsterdam in 1948, debated vigorously the Christian witness *vis-à-vis* 'the disorder of society,' and came out with the injunction that

> The Christian churches should reject the ideologies of both communism and laissez-faire capitalism, and should seek to draw men away from the false assumption that these extremes are the only alternatives. Each has made promises which it could not redeem. Communist ideology puts the emphasis upon economic justice, and promises that freedom will come automatically after the comple-

tion of the revolution. Capitalism puts the emphasis upon freedom, and promises that justice will follow as a by-product of free enterprise; that too, is an ideology which has been proved false. It is the responsibility of Christians to seek new, creative solutions which [will?] never allow either justice or freedom to destroy the other.

It is not to be pretended that such religious answers to man's social problems ever have been infallible. Amos was trying to redeem a new and oppressive social order merely by rejecting it in favor of an ancient social pattern. Micah thought there would be more freedom for farmers if there were no big cities, quite forgetting where the farmer has to sell his crops. St. Thomas lived in a setting of class separation which knew nothing of democracy. Pius XI was politically influenced not only by his residence in Mussolini's Rome (until the Concordat of 1929 made the Vatican technically an independent state, and practically much more nearly dependent on Fascism), but also by his having been Papal Nuncio in Warsaw when it was threatened by the Bolshevik march of 1920. The present writer is not altogether happy about the World Council's pronouncement just quoted, for (being an Adam Smithian) he is far less afraid of true laissez-faire capitalism than he is of capitalism made dictatorial by cartels, or by government support of selected enterprises through subsidies and tariffs.

The point is not that religious people have had all the right social answers. It is that they not only have persisted in asking many of the essential social questions, but also that such answers as they have made have spoken neither for reaction nor for indifference, but precisely for active social concern and for creative human living. Indeed, the charge of social unconsciousness leveled at religion from the left has been in our time at least balanced by the furious accusations of social radicalism that have come from the right. Thus the Church has found itself damned at once for social action and for social inaction. Perhaps the opposing camps of negative critics would do well to compare notes, and to learn each from the other. But frankness must say that those who damn the Church of today for being socially aware have much more evidence on their side than have those who think it socially inert.

There are many of us who do not believe that religious institutions as such should take specific positions on specific issues of public policy and action; and that not because we discount freedom of utterance, but because we cherish it. We want each churchman (and each non-churchman) to arrive at his own social judgments, and to contend for them on his own responsibility through the appropriate agencies of social, political, and economic action. The history of the Church when it has tried to be itself a political force is not wholly a happy one, whether seen in the mediaeval clashes between Pope and Emperor, or in the recent misadventures of American Protestants anent prohibition. Nor is there reason to suppose that any single Christian, or any group of Christians, has all the sound and workable answers to the intricate technical questions of our modern society. Social and economic usefulness requires social and economic competence, inside the Church no less than outside; and full social and economic competence seldom characterizes a body of convention delegates, whether Church or lodge or Legion. There is and there must be room for personal decision among procedures. There is everlasting necessity that each man shall decide among procedures in the light of principle.

What religion can do, and what ever it has been doing, is to test man's behavior by higher standards than man's own, and to provide the driving motive of idealism for each man's own efforts to find ways of controlling our social bewilderments. The Church has not been 'an abstract being, squatting down somewhere outside the world.' It has been in the world of men, and throughout the centuries its people have seen the world in clarity and mankind with persisting concern. A sober estimate of the evidence compels the conclusion that no force in Western history has done more than have our religious institutions to bring the ideal into contact with the actual; that no force has done it more earnestly, more honestly, more effectively, or with less of selfish interest. Those who think religion socially unconscious need first to become conscious of what religion has done in society, and for it. Then they may be of some use in helping religion to do its social work still better.

SUPERSTITION NO. 8

that ideals are impractical

⊏⊨ Johnnie, it is alleged, came home much the worse for wear; but mumbling the routine 'Y'orter see the other guy.' His mother, duly shocked, protested, 'Don't you know the Bible says when someone hits you on one cheek, you should turn to him the other too?' 'Yeah,' came back Johnnie; 'but this guy, he hit me on the nose.'

That story no doubt is worth a chuckle; yet our chuckling at it has its disturbing side. What we tell ourselves when we laugh with young Johnnie is that maybe we don't have to take Jesus' ethics very seriously. They sound fine, but they simply aren't practical. And so, sharing in Johnnie's experience, as so often we do, we are no little relieved to be able to share his conclusion.

Said G. K. Chesterton, 'Christianity has not been tried, and found wanting. It has been found difficult, and not tried.' This of course is hyperbole, but it is hyperbole with a manifest core of truth. The Sermon on the Mount is read more often than it is heard, and heard much more often than it is heeded. Many more have professed allegiance to the Christ than have obeyed the injunctions which the Gospels attribute to him. A young Turk, leaning with me on the ship's rail as we steamed up the Bosphorus, remarked, 'The theoretical difference between your religion and mine is that my prophet permitted violence, and yours did not; and practically, sir, there is no difference.'

After long and sad acquaintance with so many who call Jesus 'Lord' without any thought of doing the things that he said, it is almost a relief to meet those who frankly confess that the Christian ethic is too hard for them, and the command of the Christ beyond their possible performance. The business man who is convinced that the Golden Rule is no guide for successful buying and selling, and who frankly says so, is a more attractive and a healthier animal than the Uriah Heep who professes fidelity while practising fraud. Even the young sophisticate who holds morals to be not mores but folkways, and who on that basis argues eagerly for his own amoralism, seems refreshingly more honest than the 'converted' youth whose religion fulfills itself in emotion without visible effect on his behavior.

We need not spend time condemning the hypocrite. He has been a stock villain since long before the dawn of Christianity, and he grows no more attractive as the centuries pass. The religious and the irreligious are fully at one in despising him who claims to be something when he is nothing. When we recognize him, we are rid of him: and good riddance it is.

Nor shall I elaborate my applause for the honest dissenter, even when his honesty is beyond dispute. Some there are of course who are not quite honest even in their rejection, who sedulously rationalize their fear of personal inconvenience into an aggressive denial of what really they suspect to be right. They are hypocrites too, and no whit to be preferred to those who deny only by their conduct. But there are honest disbelievers in any sort of traditional ethical value; and no greater tribute need be paid to them than frankly to admit their honesty.

Yet their approach to life surely is oversimplified. How many of the inherited values actually persist in them, effectively even though unconsciously? Are they really as emancipated from their early moral training as they suppose? How far is the very chance they have to live their personal anarchism dependent on obedience to statute or moral law on the part of the more innocent souls among whom they are living? Individual freedom, they will do well to remember, usually is more readily achieved within social order than ever it can be under generalized chaos.

These, however, are only minor challenges, secondary evidences of the infinite complexity of the problem. To say that ideals are impractical, sounding simple, turns out immediately to be too simple, since it by no means disposes of the presence in life of the values it negates in words. To say that ideals are wholly practicable sounds simple too; and without much sharper definition is functionally meaningless. What ideals are we talking about? How shall we select among the innumerable ideals (including that of 'practicality') which compete for our attention and acceptance? And once we have found ideals which we are willing to call our own, what is the procedure for putting them into effect?

Here already are more questions than this chapter can answer, or this author; but at least some further discussion of them seems to be indicated. The place in which to look for ideals is the only one in which we can look: that is, within the culture patterns we have known and in which we have lived. For members of Western society, this means essentially the Hebrew-Christian tradition. What ideals have characterized this heritage of ours? How relevant are they for today? Can we live by them in the second half of the twentieth century?

Of course one may not exclude the possibility that acquaintance with another culture, such as the Arab or the Chinese, may lead a Westerner to decide that the ideals of Islam or of Confucianism are superior for him. A very distant relative of mine, now gone to his Paradise, used to be described as the leading English Muslim; but it was commonly said of him that, had he been born in Arabia, he would indubitably have become the leading Arab Christian. The statistical incidence of this sort of thing in our society, however, is so slight that for practical purposes it may be set aside. In general, too, much that is to be said about the relevance of the ideals transmitted within our tradition will apply *pari passu* to those which have been developed in others of the great heritages of humankind.

The simplest positive answer within the Western framework, and not an uncommon one, is to say that the Scriptures contain

the moral law, and that their authority is final. Thus for the Jew
the Torah, with the Ten Commandments as a selected summary, is fundamental. For the Christian there are to be added the
teachings of Jesus, centrally represented in the Sermon on the
Mount. We have, therefore, says this view, our obligations clearly
marked out for us. All we have to do is to obey.

This simplicity, however, is deceptive. The Ten Commandments, sounding (and quite possibly being) one of the most direct and least confusing of moral codes, turn out on examination
to raise a number of subtle questions. Already, in another connection, we have noted the Jewish use of the second commandment (the third, by the way, in their reckoning) as a prohibition
of any representational art work. No Christian tradition ever
has understood this injunction in this way; and there is a good
deal of evidence that the interpretation among the Hebrew people was extremely flexible. The decorations of Solomon's temple
are reported to have included lions, oxen, and cherubim; and
neither the early narrative in Kings nor the later rewriting in
Chronicles seems to regard their making as a violation of the Law.
Much later, probably in early Christian times, there was built in
the city of Jerash in Transjordania a Jewish Synagogue whose mosaic floor pictured Noah, his ark, his whole family, and a very engaging variety of animals.

The prohibition of taking 'the name of the Lord thy God in
vain' also has a fascinating history. There is reason to suppose
that originally it meant, 'Thou shalt not call on the Lord when
thou art empty-handed'; or, as we would say, there should be no
church service without the taking of a collection. But in Judaism
this came to mean that one should not pronounce the Lord's
personal name at all. That name, represented by the characters
JHVH, was so long unused orally that its proper vocalization is
not certainly known; and in speech there was always substituted
for it, as there is in Jewish services to this day, the generic
Adonai, 'Lord.' This is the source of our use of that term in the
'King James' version, wherever the Hebrew text has the sacred
JHVH. The 'Jehovah' of the American Standard revision is

a mongrel word, being composed of the consonants JHVH and the (slightly modified) vowels of *Adonai*.

Later on there was a shifting of attention to the matter of oaths in the context of good faith. As Philo Judaeus of Alexandria put it in his commentary on the Decalogue, 'Next to not swearing at all, the second best thing is to keep one's oath.' Finally there developed, both in Judaism and in Christianity, the familiar use of this commandment as an injunction against profanity. This would be simpler to deal with if our various linguistic and local traditions could achieve any unanimity as to what words are profane and what aren't. (The list is long; but note, for example, devil and *diable*, O God and O gosh, 'Jesus' and 'gee whizz,' and the thundering difference between British and American reactions to what for me is the still unutterable 'bloody.')

A much more important commandment, but one no more easy to pin down as to its precise significance, is 'Thou shalt not kill.' 'Thou shalt not kill' what? Animals? Some conscientious vegetarians thus have maintained, but it is Jainism rather than either Judaism or Christianity that has taken this position authoritatively; and of course quite without reference to the Jewish Decalogue. National enemies? Manifestly the dominant Jewish judgment never thought of forbidding the slaying of the nation's foes in battle; and so if a Christian concludes that this commandment requires absolute pacifism, he actually is creating a new commandment in the light of his own chosen values. Does this word forbid capital punishment? Again Biblical Judaism seems to have encouraged no such idea; and they who would answer 'yes' to the question do so chiefly because on other grounds they think capital punishment morally wrong, or practically ineffective, or both.

Nor is the 'simple Gospel' of Jesus wholly simple when we settle down to analyze it. The general impact of the Sermon on the Mount indeed is clear: an emphasis on human value rather than formal law, on inner attitude rather than outward conformity. But an enquiry into the details, and into their application in practice, raises questions of no slight complexity.

What is the Christian ethic with regard to divorce? The Roman tradition, treating as authoritative the dicta as quoted in St. Mark x and St. Luke xvi, says that no divorce ever is permissible. The Anglican view (has it anything to do with the personal history of Henry VIII?) has depended rather on the Gospel according to St. Matthew, which both in chapter v and in chapter xix permits an exception for the single cause of adultery. In the American scene one Church after another has modified its rules about the remarriage of divorced persons, until today there are few legally permissible marriages that are firmly prohibited by any Church other than the Roman, and probably none whose parties cannot find some minister of recognized standing to bless it. Even Roman usage, still officially repudiating any divorce whatever, has seemed recently to broaden the scope of 'annulment' far beyond its customary meaning. At the moment I am not arguing either for or against the permissibility of divorce to a Christian. I am only pointing out that any Christian who thinks any divorce permissible is flatly rejecting the specific words of the early Gospel tradition.

A cognate matter is that of personal sexual morality. Only the ultra-sophisticates of our time admit that they do not regard adultery as a serious offence. Is it possible, however, for anyone to take literally the sentence, 'Whosoever looketh on a woman to lust after her hath committed adultery with her already in his heart'? If we try to take this at face value, and to condemn any extra-marital sexual inclination as being sin in itself, we are identifying the sin with the temptation, the biological impulse with the conscious yielding to it. Mark Twain, in 'The Man Who Corrupted Hadleyburg,' did a thorough job of challenging the cognate 'Lead us not into temptation'; and Mr. Clemens' strictures on a literal treatment of that petition will appeal to many a Christian, probably to most, as extremely well taken. Certainly the writer of the letter to the Hebrews regarded temptation as normal human experience, and spoke hopefully of its conquest rather than at all of its abolition. Indeed, he insisted that Jesus himself 'was tempted in all points like as we are, yet without sin.'

Unquestionably the principal ethical issue that is being fought out among Christians today is that of pacifism. The historic Quaker 'witness,' long shared by the Mennonites and related groups, has gained many adherents in Christian fellowships other than the 'peace Churches.' It was only by the margin of a single vote among some eight hundred that the Methodist General Conference of 1942 expressed its assent to American participation in the war; and numerically (though of course not as to percentage within the several denominations) the Methodist conscientious objectors to the draft led the members of all other communions. The Korean war has revived the disputing of the early 1940's, and without bringing us at all nearer to agreement.

Proof-texting on this problem is utterly hopeless, whether one uses the whole Bible as a quarry or confines himself to the recorded sayings of Jesus. Probably a sound critical estimate of the New Testament sources would drive us to say, 'Yes, Jesus was a pacifist.' Immediately, however, many of us will go on to add sentences beginning with 'But.' Among those 'buts' are the early Christian assumption that the end of the world was near, with the consequent identification of the ethic as one designed for the interim; the fact that any sort of armed revolt against Rome was foredoomed to defeat, as the events of the years 68–70 were so clearly to demonstrate; and the question as to whether in a final estimate of values the death of the human body is so grave a tragedy as the destruction of the human spirit.

It is then a matter of debate whether the situation which Jesus faced was exactly comparable with ours, and whether, therefore, his conclusion should be used to determine our own. What are we to think, or to do, about those issues in our modern society which simply have no recognizable parallels in Biblical times? Does the Hebrew-Christian tradition, for example, support free enterprise? Or does it require us to adhere to the Fair Deal? Or to socialism?

In such matters as these the 'back to Jesus' answer is no answer at all. Jesus never saw a modern factory, never heard of corporate securities, never met a union organizer or a bank president. Only the most naïve will try here to line Jesus up on one side or the other, as of course some have tried, and on both sides. The fact is that the specifics of the Biblical ethic apply to the Israelite nation and to the Hellenistic world under Rome. Where we have to deal with entirely new social phenomena we have no ancient prescription, not even a difficult and puzzling one, to direct us.

The obvious recourse then is to general principles, which should be applicable to all situations at all times. Does the Bible give us these? When from specifics we turn to generalizations we find ourselves indeed with less of specific confusion, but even more of general uncertainty. Jesus' most famous inclusive declarations are the Golden Rule and the Summary of the Law. 'All things whatsoever ye would that men should do to you, do ye even so to them.' As a guide in principle that is unquestionably helpful; but since we want so many different things ourselves, even our complete obedience to this rule would mean our doing many very different things to and for others, and quite possibly things that some of the others might not like at all. 'Thou shalt love the Lord thy God. . . . Thou shalt love thy neighbour as thyself.' Again and again we read this summary in the Communion Office, and always it serves to remind us of the fact that life has its basic obligations for us. But what those obligations are in detail can be determined only as we select among innumerable varieties of detailed interpretation and application.

The famous 'categorical imperative' of Immanuel Kant, which clearly is akin to the Golden Rule, also attempts to provide a total guide for conduct. 'So act,' says the analyst of the practical reason, 'as if the maxim from which you act were to become through your will a universal law of nature.' But little Johnnie, in the episode with which this chapter began, has effectively disposed of this as an infallible criterion. Each of us, accepting it in theory as we all do whether or not we ever heard it phrased, proceeds immediately to vitiate it by his own certainty that no one else ever faced quite his set of circumstances. 'If anyone else were as hungry as I,' we say, 'it would be all right for him to steal too. If anyone else needed a passing grade as badly, he couldn't be blamed for cheating. If anyone else were as much in love as I am, he couldn't be expected to worry about breaking up a marriage that mattered much less than such love.'

It follows from all these perplexing considerations that a high degree of relativism, and relativism personal as well as cultural, has to be admitted as existing within the ethical scene. Before we leap to the conclusion of absolute anarchy, however, we shall do well to notice something of what has been done in the world by those who have chosen absolutely to conform to some of the ethical standards that history has produced. Absolute poverty, for example, not even the Roman Church regards as desirable for everyone. Yet the absolute personal poverty of the religious orders has produced some of the most magnificent human living that mankind ever has observed, and some of the genuinely happiest. Not even the Church requires celibacy of all its adherents. Yet again the sublimation achieved by the clergy and by the religious has been richly productive in creative service both humane and artistic; and again to the full contentment of men and women for whom this has been the compelling personal ideal.

The very definition of 'absolute' pacifism is hard to make; for, as a leading American pacifist remarked to me, the specific point of pacifist resistance to conscription is a matter of one's choosing a particular symbol. It is true too that the pacifist witness of the Quakers, always standing in a curious antinomy with the Friends' insistence on the primacy of the Inner Light, has broken down into the choosing of various points all along the vast distance from full participation in war to flat refusal to register under the Selective Service Act. Nevertheless, with all this evident inconsistency, Quakerism has made its impact on the world so unmistakably as to merit and to gain the applause of count-

less people who share not at all in the historic Quaker judgments. No one can discount the work of the American Friends'
Service Committee; and none can think to dissociate that work
from the ideals that the Friends chose so long ago and that their
children have maintained in their own several ways.

Albert Schweitzer has been so much publicized in recent years
that he may have lost some force as an illustration. The very
fact that his story is so well known, however, and that it has
made such a widespread impression, reënforces the judgment that
absolute adherence to one's chosen ideals is worth something to
the individual and to mankind. Indeed, Dr. Schweitzer's may be
a particularly good case to examine, because it is so perfect an illustration of an individual's choosing a unique set of values because he has had a unique background of experience. Here is a
man committed to the most rigorous Biblical scholarship, to the
highest standards of musical performance, and withal to the
hardest of labor in his missionary hospital in Africa. All these are
ideals, his own ideals; and none will venture to say that they
have proved impractical in him.

The resolution of our problem has to be sought along such
lines as these. No sort of critical judgment, historical or practical, will be content with any external rule as a sufficient expression of the ideal for any man or woman. Schweitzer himself, manifestly expressing the central Christian ethic in his own living, is
of all men the most responsible for developing the theory that
Jesus' moral patterns were designed not for the long reach of
history but for a brief period of anticipation before the end of
the world. There is no quick summary available to solve our
problems of ethical choice. There is rather a much heavier responsibility, and a much more challenging one, to work out our own
ideals in infinite detail with reference to the world that now
is, and against the background of what we may identify as the
best guidance that we can secure.

What religion has to say on this point is that the choice of the
ideal must be itself an ideal one, made in terms of values honestly

selected and accepted, and maintained unflinchingly whatever may be the result. The discovery of the absolute right is, humanly speaking, inevitably fragmentary, and never is to be guaranteed by any external proof. Thus one of us will discover this fragment of eternal rightness, and another of us quite a different fragment. Each of our great religious traditions has its own preferences, its own emphases, its own efforts to reflect an absolute which finally is beyond human ken.

The absoluteness is not in the naming of the ideal, but in the living of it. Truly religious people may differ hopelessly as to whether war, or liquor, or socialism, or protective tariffs, can be thought compatible with Christian standards. Every truly religious person, however, will be absolutely honest in his selection of the best as best he can find it: which means selection of the ideal without rationalizing, without any kind of self-deception, without self-seeking most of all. Every truly religious person also will be an absolutist in holding to the ideal which he has chosen, so long as in moral absoluteness it commands his highest judgment, whatever may be the cost to him individually or whatever may be the measurable result in the social scene.

A corollary to this, and one not to be avoided, is that the most effective choosing of ideals, and the most effective living by them, depend not only upon sincerity of purpose, but also upon the individual's degree of intelligence and upon his quantity of information. This does not mean, obviously and lamentably, that the most intelligent and the best informed people either have found the best ideals in life, or that they obey them the most truly. It does mean that they have a better chance on both counts, and therefore a greater responsibility. 'Unto whomsoever much is given, of him shall be much required.'

One last challenge of 'practicality' is requisite. Certainly one's ideals must be related to the existing world; and, as we have seen, they cannot be selected otherwhere than from the world that one has known. But the practicality of pragmatism is at the

other pole from the religious choosing of values. Pragmatism
operates by definition in the realm of fact, and its validation is in
terms of evidence and demonstration. The religious ideal, to be
religious, must go beyond pragmatism in its ethic just as it goes
beyond science in its metaphysic. The danger which religion sees
in pragmatism is not in its good sense, but in its lack of ultimate
sensitivity; and in its consequently strong tendency never to
fight a hopeless battle, never to embrace a visibly losing cause.

In a sense religious ideals always must be 'impractical,' if practicality is to be tested by objective success. This is not a question of personal victory or comfort or satisfaction only. It is
much more significantly the question of what chances the
ideal may be thought to have in the 'practical' world. For religious faith this criterion, though often helpful on the lower
level of tactics, is utterly irrelevant to the choosing of values.
We all shall agree that what is, is not enough to claim our loyalty. We need, however, to rise beyond interest in what we suppose can be, to final and absolute allegiance to what we are convinced ought to be. 'It is not necessary to succeed,' said William
the Silent in one of his rare utterances, 'in order to persevere.
It is not necessary to hope in order to endure.' In even more
'practical' vein the Prince of Orange remarked, 'There is one certain means by which I can be sure never to see my country's ruin
—I will die in the last ditch.'

Thus the view that ideals are impractical is sound enough, and
indeed is absolutely essential to maintain, if this is understood to
mean that practicality in visible outcome is not the measure
by which ideals are to be chosen. It is false, however, blatantly
false, damningly false, if it represents the judgment that ideals
cannot be lived. Countless men and women have shown that they
can be lived, from the heroes of the faith who are listed in Eccle-
siasticus xliv and Hebrews xi through all the hosts of their successors in the ages since, and even in this devil's world that is
our own. We have admitted that the reported words of Jesus are
not self-interpreting ideals in themselves. We nonetheless are

driven always to recognize that the ideals which Jesus chose for himself, against a Jewish background and under the rule of Rome, he lived out fully even unto death.

Here once more the book of Job is to the point. It not only admits, but flatly asserts, that no one has gained visible benefit from Job's righteousness, least of all Job. Job's friends are rational men, eminently practical men: pragmatists every one of them. They measure by results, and so they reject Job's whole position. And they are so evidently wrong, so completely and invincibly wrong. He who is right in this dispute is he who has no practical argument at all to offer, no hope in this world or the next: no practical argument, that is, except his quiet purpose to practise the right as he sees it, no hope but his determination to maintain his chosen ideal. Job provides the philosophical argument for the 'impractical ideal' made real, and Jesus its compelling demonstration.

The ideal thus stubbornly pursues every one of us; and especially those who by ability, or training, or expert knowledge, are qualified intellectually to select among varieties and actively to achieve fulfilment. The ideal is practical, not for its outward victory but for its inner living, for everyone who has the capacity to discriminate and the courage to decide. That then includes the business man, whose balance sheet never can be accepted by religion as the measure of his moral obligation. It includes also the intellectual, whose very power to obfuscate issues marks his skill to clarify them. The ideal is hard to find, and harder to make real in life. Is not that sufficient challenge to the capable to try to find it, and to the brave to try to live it?

SUPERSTITION NO. 9

*that values can be achieved
and maintained in isolation*

Here we come to the case of those who do not profess irreligion as such, but who (as herein will be argued) effectively practise irreligion by cutting themselves off from the organized fellowship of religious people. 'I can be religious,' the argument goes, 'without bothering with the Church. I can live a moral life in my home and in my business. I can think better alone than I can in a crowd. I can worship God in the hills or by the sea. Why should I go to tiresome services, and listen to dull sermons, when my religion is complete without the need of anything of that sort?'

The summary answer to all this is the one Jesus made to some men who were taking exactly the opposite point of view. The scribes and Pharisees were very much concerned to carry out their formal religious duties, even to the point of setting aside for the Temple the tenth part of the produce of their herb gardens; but, said Jesus, they had omitted 'the weightier matters of the law, judgment, mercy, and faith.' 'These,' he concluded, 'ought ye to have done, and not to leave the other undone.'

For the moment let us concede the positives which our friends assert of themselves. Let us suppose that they have not neglected judgment, mercy, and faith. Let us admit that they live what is recognized as a decent life, that they have a reverent approach to the God of nature, that their thought about religion is serious and honest. These things are good, and they should be included in every religious life. These, therefore, rightly are done. But what about the things that have been left undone? Are they quite as unimportant, quite as trivial, as has been alleged?

The first question that presents itself is that of the origin of these personal values with which their holders are so fully content. What is the measure of a personal 'moral life' in our society? With all the shifts in detailed interpretation noted in the preceding chapter, with all the changes brought about by change in social situations, the central ethical emphases of the Hebrew-Christian tradition are clear enough to make it evident that they have set the accepted standards of individual behavior: honesty, hard work, family loyalty, a measure of kindness. How, again, did our friend happen to find his God in the heavens or upon the mountains? He may or may not read the Psalms, but inescapably he borrows from them. (Perhaps he borrows *via* Wordsworth, which makes him the more sentimental and appreciably the less religious; but this distinction he keeps outside the range of his notice.) Where, finally, did he get the ideas he reworks, or the books that he reads for further stimulus? The ancestry of the books and the ideas is evident in their character: again the heritage of Hebrew-Christianity.

The extent to which our culture is suffused with the religious traditions of Israel and of Western Europe has been discussed at length in an earlier chapter. There our concern was chiefly with those who, because of secularity in our prevailing ways of education, never have received the cultural bequest which is rightfully theirs. Now we are dealing with a somewhat different group: that whose members, owing the debt because they have benefited by the good received, deny it in their failure to realize who their benefactors have been.

It is clear enough, at least in theory, that the individual legatee can seize his inheritance, take it to himself, and enjoy its blessings, while remaining quite alone. He learned the tradition in school, he can read the Psalms for inspiration and other books for knowledge, he can unite his early education and his current thinking to produce for himself new formulations which he finds interesting and satisfying. This is precisely what he claims to be possible, because he is convinced that he has done it. And in it he is wholly satisfied.

At the risk of disturbing the peace he so happily has gained, we must ask him now how far this pleasant theory really works out in practice. There are a number of practical questions that demand to be raised. For example, what procedure does this man use to check on his morality, first as to its specific relevance to the modern scene, and then as to the stability with which actually he maintains his own ethical course? How often actually does he think of God on a Sierra Club trip, and what sort of prayer does he usually offer when he is fishing? What criteria does he employ to test the validity of his own thinking, or the validity of argument in the books that he reads?

The tradition of religious faith is not a static entity, completed when the Scriptural canon was established, or when the now middle-aged managed at last to escape from regular Sunday School attendance. The concepts of theology are not closed, the structure of an ethical system needs continually to be reëxamined in the light of new situations, the experience of worship is something different in community from what it is in solitude. What all this means is that the communion of saints, which produced the riches that this man treasures, has not gone out of business. It still is producing; and if he does not know what its products are today, he is (oh, how this will upset him!) simply out-of-date.

The religious institutions of our society are by far the oldest social organisms now in existence, much older than the political entities, and having outlived countless changing imperial and national powers. The Church of Jesus Christ carries on today, well into its twentieth successive century, the same work of trying to interpret the issues of life, the same adventure of seeking to solve the riddles of the universe, the same service of inspiration to its people, in which it has engaged from the beginning, and by which it created the values which now our solitary thinks to hug to himself. If, however, he ignores the continuing creativity of the Church, he is clinging to a static revelation rather than sharing in a growing one. It has to be granted that many within the Church do not quite succeed in keeping intellectual and moral pace with the Church's growing discoveries and realizations. It is evident, however, that they have a far better chance to keep up than does he who hears nothing at all of what is going on.

The 'decent life' cliché, for example, all too commonly reflects the purely individual ethic of early Protestantism, without any recognition either of the social urgency of the Hebrew prophets and the communal spirit of mediaeval Christianity, on the one hand, or of today's vital attempts to relate religious values to the workings of our industrial economy, on the other. Our fugitive from fellowship no doubt refrains from killing, from stealing, perhaps even from malevolence. He pays his bills, he gives his secretary the prevailing salary for her job category, he hands the office boy a bit of folding money for Christmas. These things ought he to do; but there are other things he may be leaving undone because they never have been brought to his attention.

Has it occurred to him that the 'decent life' in this generation scarcely is complete without recognizing not only the need of the office boy for some extra Christmas cash, but also the continuing need of our economy to keep prices stable enough so that the middle class will not be quite wiped out? No doubt he gets excited about his taxes; but he may be quite startled at the suggestion that one's judgment about the tax system, in terms of its social effects, ought to be determined in the light of fundamental moral value. He grumbles to the secretary, even though usually he brags to his friends, about the growing size of her semi-monthly check; yet commonly he is unaware equally of the relevance of her buying power to the general success of business, a purely mathematical relationship, and of the relevance of her income to her personal adjustment, which is an ethical and finally a religious consideration.

I have alluded to the contradictory charges against the Church which are made by those who think it does too little in the social realm and by those who think it does too much. Our present problem character does not fit exactly into either of these categories, but he too needs some education. His weakness is that, while he sees the bearing of religious judgments on his personal financial probity, he fails altogether to carry the logic through to the larger realms of business and industrial procedure. Judgment, mercy, and faith are equally demanding on every level; and to adhere to them only in the narrowed circle of the individual's behavior is to deny them in the wider reaches of man's experience in a total community. The first challenge, then, to the person who believes he can be moral without formal religious contacts is to ask him how far his morality reaches. If he will investigate, he is likely to find that religion holds it should reach much further.

Akin to the failure to see the wider relevance of ethical judgments in the world is the unwillingness to admit that one needs support from others in the fulfillment of his own moral obligations. This consideration appears at two noticeable points: that of aid and encouragement in maintaining a personal code, and that of the power of unity in achieving a social goal. As to the personal side, what has happened frequently in our modern urban communities has been the substitution of the luncheon club for the Church as a source of strength and comfort to the individual. Actually any Rotarian or Kiwanian who denies the value of fellowship in the Church is hopelessly self-contradictory. What really he is saying is that he prefers the club to the Church, whether because of its mood or because of its particular morals. Those morals, we should note, while of the highest standard in the personal area, commonly represent just the individualist ethic that was the mark of Puritanism; and one is driven to suspect that the preference for club over Church may exist because the club makes fewer suggestions that are upsetting to personal satisfaction in an old and unexamined mode of conduct.

The luncheon clubber who denies the claims of the Church, while confessing allegiance to the Christian ideal, thus stands convicted of at least a measure of dishonesty in his profession. His objection is not to association, which he seeks in this other setting. It would seem then that he must be governing his choice by considerations of content; and whether that content be individually or socially centered, it never is quite the same in a group of men gathered because of business association as it is in a fellowship whose common concern is the realization of the ultimate values of all of human experience.

The further step of coöperation as a multiplier of individual usefulness also characterizes the luncheon club to some extent; and I have no purpose to deny the valuable public services which many of the clubs have rendered, and the genuine generosity with which some of them have contributed time and money to the development of programs of welfare in their communities. The clubs now are national and international too, and they have made enough impact on the world to become in themselves a major issue for Roman Catholic policy. Here again, however, the Church is a far greater institution than is the luncheon club, much more truly international, much more inclusive in its interests, in its services, and in its personnel. If one believes he should support the program of his club, his only tenable reason for refusing to support the program of the greater social servant which is the Church is that he really isn't for the Church's program. This is his privilege, if he wishes to take it. All I am asking is that he shall not disguise from himself the real reason for his reluctance to share in the enterprise of the Christian fellowship.

None of this luncheon club analogy applies to the genuine re-cluse. He may really dislike groups of people all of the time, as all of us do some of the time. Still the needs that luncheon club and Church both attempt to meet exist in him, and for him. Every one of us holds more sincerely to his ideals when he knows that others grasp them too, than when he withdraws and seeks to maintain them quite alone. Every one of us is a helpless animal-cule in the whirling social maelstrom, rather than a creator of order within it, unless and until he joins his strength with that of others to drive toward a chosen goal. Anchoritism character-ized very early Christianity; but soon, and inevitably, it yielded to the creation of fellowship even among those whose religion called on them to withdraw from the world. *A fortiori*, fellow-ship is essential to personal completeness for us who are in the world: fellowship with those who are like-minded and like-hearted. It follows, then, that he who claims a like mind and heart with the Church belongs in it, and not in the weakness and ineffectiveness of solitude.

The worship cliché is similar to that of the 'decent life.' Of course it is possible to worship God on the mountain top. It is possible to worship God also on the polo field, or driving along the highway, or in a baseball park. It is likely that God has been truly worshipped in all of these places. If, however, we raise the question of statistical probability, we scarcely shall maintain that the worship of God is quite as frequent here as it is in the houses built in his honor and devoted to his praise. I have told elsewhere the story of the father who said, 'Come on, we can sing hymns on the beach,' to whom the little girl replied, 'But we won't, will we?' We can. But do we?

Again the relevance is both personal and social. Rare is the in-dividual who can maintain his devotional exercise always alone, without any stimulus from those who share his values of devo-tion. Nor can individual devotion provide all the experience that comes to them who participate, willingly and purposefully, in the religious symbols of a religious community. For the individual, every value he can get alone (except the value of solitude itself) is also available when others are present, for he can still invite his spirit; and there are other values, too, which the other people provide, in the realization of their joining with him in the quest for touch with ultimate meaning and ultimate life.

It is just a little difficult to be polite about this popular way of trying to justify non-attendance at services of worship. I suggest that it is a reasonable supposition that the people who go to church get quite as much out of the worship of God in nature as do those whose temple is the forest only. In point of fact the nature-is-enough approach is likely to be utterly sentimental, without either the moral content or the personal consecration that are essential to worship rightly so called. This is why Wordsworth is so inferior to the ancient Psalmists. He, as they, saw God in the starry heavens above; but they were the ones who knew this God to be present also in the moral law. Much current worship of 'God in nature' is nothing more than an unreflective and unmoral pantheism; and it will not be corrected until the God of physical nature is met also among those other creations of his whom we know as men and women.

This may be the point at which to comment on the 'tiresome service and dull sermon' routine. The first question to be asked of those who make this complaint is the same one that many pages ago was addressed to those who suppose religion has not changed since their school days: 'Just how long is it, sir, since you went to church?' That there are tiresome services and dull sermons is not to be denied, especially by an author who has conducted the former and preached the latter, more times than he is willing to remember. But the tiresomeness of the service is subjective as well as objective; and a certain readiness to get something out of the service is a remarkable specific for the malady of getting nothing out of it. The same is true even of the sermon, which at its worst ought to start some significant train of thought in minds fully aware of their own superiority to that with which the unfortunate preacher is endowed.

Actually, however, the charge usually lacks point because it is made by those who have no evidence to present. The recent development in liturgics, in all the major Protestant denominations, has made the services of worship more beautiful in form and greatly richer in meaning. The quality of preaching certainly is uneven; but a great deal of it is informed and thoughtful, and some of it is creative and inspiring. If our friend doesn't like artichokes, he may eat eggplant with satisfaction; and if he doesn't like one church, he has at least as wide a field of option open to him among churches as he has among comestibles. How many of them has he sampled enough to know how they taste?

I am willing also to defend the proposition that one who professes faith in the values of religion ought to align himself with that religious fellowship which comes the nearest to expressing his values, even though he may be bored more often than he is inspired, and even though he knows he could sing better than the choir and speak better than the minister. The immediate fellowship is there, despite the inadequacy of its articulate expression. The worldwide fellowship is there, in the outreach of the Church to all mankind. The opportunity of service is there, far more broadly and far more intensively than in any of those surrogates for the Church that our society has invented in these secular times. 'He that is not with me is against me; and he that gathereth not with me scattereth abroad.' It is time that they who say they are for what the churches are for, should prove their good faith by joining in the work that the churches are doing.

A final challenge here is that of the obligation of the negative critic to do something positive toward improvement. The weaker the church is, the more strength it needs. The poorer its thinking, the richer the service a clear mind can render in it. The greater the percentage of hypocrites in the congregation, the larger the difference the adding of one honest man will make. But it is precisely honesty that is at issue. To one who used the 'hypocrite' argument, an old parson is said to have replied, 'Then come along, my friend; there's always room for one more.' To say that one adheres to Christian values, and then to refuse to have any share in the institution that has preserved those values, and that today is struggling to make them ever more real among men, is hypocrisy indeed.

The central issue of this chapter is simply that of the place of institutions in human life. Always there is tension between the individual and the group, and almost inevitably there is tension, too, between any idea and the human organization that is created to maintain and promote the idea. The pendulum swings, for the person and for the society, back and forth between individual independence and social support, between freedom and order.

Three factors in particular have worked to suspend the typical American of our day long at the independent end of the curve. In general we still hold strongly, if a trifle impractically, to the adventuring mood of the first colonists of Jamestown, to the frontier tradition of the pioneers in Kentucky. With special reference to the Church, an early force making for individual detachment was the fact, already noted in another connection, that our first and definitive colonization occurred just at the time of the break with Rome. The survival of this separatist mood made itself fully apparent in the innumerable further divisions that sturdy individuals then brought about within American Protestantism, ultimately to the grave weakening of the religious forces of our country. Most recently, and within the Church itself, the discovery of the Hebrew prophets has led to an enthusiasm for personal revolt against a religious institution supposed to be reactionary past hope.

Thus the modern American, predisposed anyway to suspect formal organizations and very sure of his ability to stand on his own feet, has heard even churchmen implying that the Church doesn't matter: that prophets rather than priests convey the truth of God, that Micah's prediction that the temple would be destroyed was more religious than Zechariah's urgency that it should be rebuilt, that Amos was a great prophet when he assailed the priesthood, and 'Malachi' a decadent one when he

supported it. What many of the enthusiasts about early proph-
etism have not noted, and what, therefore, the layman has
not had a chance to hear, is that it was precisely the later religious institution of Judaism that preserved the writings of
those who so vigorously had attacked the institution in its earlier days.

Amos and Micah, Hosea and Isaiah, had lived and spoken when
the two Hebrew nations still were going concerns. They saw
faults in the existing structures, and courageously they condemned the faults as they saw them. Ezekiel and 'Malachi,'
Haggai and Zechariah, wrote after both the nations had fallen.
Instead of damning, therefore, they encouraged. There was
nothing left to tear down, and so they devoted themselves to
rebuilding. With the political state of Judah wiped out, only
the institution of religion was left to keep the Jewish tradition
alive. Because the priests did keep it alive, the works of the early
prophets were treasured and recopied; and so the independent
souls of the former times were given their immortality by the
very conformists who succeeded them. And so, more im-
portantly still, the moral and spiritual ideals of these early inde-
pendents became the living bond of the continuing community of Israel.

We always shall need the free soul, the adventurer, the maver-
ick. Society needs him, and the Church needs him. We need his
vigor, his criticism, his flashes of personal inspiration. But the
greater the service he renders. the surer it is that an institution
will have to assume the task of cherishing his insights and advanc-
ing his enthusiasms. The new wine of the Christian gospel proved
too effervescent to be held in the older wineskins of the Temple and the Synagogue. Yet immediately, and perforce, the adherents of that gospel began to pour the wine into the new
bottle of the Church. Without that bottle to contain it, the
new wine of Christianity quickly would have been spilled, and
would have sunk without trace into the dust of the Hellenistic
world.

In this day of human crisis we need especially the kind of unity, the 'league offensive and defensive,' that Judaism achieved in the Temple, that the little company of Jesus' followers created in the Church, that Wesley (whose phrase I have just quoted) devised in the first Methodist societies. 'None of us liveth to himself'; and any one of us who tries to will not survive long in any usefulness to our world. To say that we can be religious without fellowship in resource is arrogantly inaccurate. To suppose that we can be religious without fellowship in service is pathetically unrealistic. He who genuinely adheres to moral values today needs all the assistance he can get, and owes all the aid that he can give.

'Morality,' a teacher of mine used to say, 'began with the organization of the first family.' The Hebrew-Christian tradition always has maintained that morality has to be thus socially defined. We are not complete persons save in a family relationship. We are not responsible citizens except as we play our part in the nation. We are not authentically religious without the expression of our religion in fellowship and through it. The bachelor and the spinster bring up no children to carry on the world's work. To the would-be bachelor in moral values, in religion, the call must be, 'Come back into the family. Then, and only then, will you have spiritual children to maintain the values you profess.'

SUPERSTITION NO. 9½

that religious people
can't have fun

⊂⊇ This last of our list of superstitions, though widely prevalent, is so trivial and baseless that it scarcely deserves ranking as a major issue. I am, therefore, numbering it not 10, but 9½.

The supposition that religious people can't have fun, accompanied by arched eyebrows when a religious person obviously does, seems to hinge on two principal judgments of the secular world. One is the tradition that religion is principally a system of taboos designed to make men and women unhappy. The other is the assumption that fun is to be identified exclusively with partying, drinking, and what is vulgarly but very accurately called 'helling around.'

That there have been historic negatives about personal behavior, both in the Jewish system and in Christian circles is manifestly true. That some of these were childish in their beginnings is possible. That many of them have been outgrown and ought promptly to be discarded is unquestionable. Before we rule them out *en masse*, however, it may be well for us to investigate their origin and purpose.

Sabbath regulations, being common to Judaism and to the British-American variety of Protestantism, provide an interesting case in point. As they were enforced in our grandparents' day (though scarcely in ours) they often seemed petty and meaningless, and therefore needlessly repressive. This is the sort of thing that happens with most laws when, through the passage of time, their original motive has become obscured and only the letter of the statute remains readily to be seen.

The reason assigned for Sabbath observance in the version of the Ten Commandments preserved in Exodus xx is a formal one, based upon the later of the two creation stories in the book of Genesis:

> For in six days the Lord made heaven and earth, the sea, and all that in them is, and rested the seventh day: wherefore the Lord blessed the sabbath day, and hallowed it.

Since the Reformed and Anglican Churches have treated this Exodus Decalogue as normative, the 'creation' basis for Sabbath rest has been uppermost in British and American thinking. The Roman Church and the Lutherans have done more wisely in reading the Commandments in Deuteronomy v, a text probably earlier and certainly more realistic. Here the reason given is one that will appeal much more to men and women of today:

> . . . that thy manservant and thy maidservant may rest as well as thou. And remember that thou wast a servant in the land of Egypt, and that the Lord thy God brought thee out thence through a mighty hand and by a stretched out arm: therefore the Lord thy God commanded thee to keep the sabbath day.

That is to say, according to this writer the keeping of the Sabbath had a dual purpose: the humanitarian one of providing regular rest for the employed (or enslaved) worker, and the moral one of reminding the comfortable that their own origins had been humble and difficult.

Wherever there is law, however, there have to be lawyers to interpret it. Rabbinic and scribal tradition worked on the applying of the rule of rest as to all possible details; and so the details rather than the intent came to the noticeable surface. When through the argument of Nicholas Bownd (A.D. 1606, in the reign of James I) something like the Jewish Sabbath became normative for the Sunday of Puritan-oriented Christians, the same process of detailed interpretation began immediately. Actually the Anglo-Saxon Christians went further than the Jews ever had, for they tended to make the day's restrictions apply not to work quite so much as to pleasure. While the Orthodox Jewish housewife would do no cooking on the Sabbath, the Christian household commonly ate particularly well on Sunday, ruling rather against any play for the children. Thus what originally was a humanitarian and an affirmative law became, as all of us born before the turn of the century will testify, an inhumane negation of all our childhood impulses and interests.

Much the same thing happened with reference to dietary regulations. The original Israelite distinction between 'clean' and 'unclean' meat no doubt had reference to what was considered appropriate for sacrifice to God. Possibly a primitive totemism was involved here, as a number of scholars have suggested. It is difficult, however, to follow the logic whereby some totem animals were freely to be eaten, and some were to be consumed only on ceremonial occasions, while others were to be abjured at all times. Whatever the motive may have been, it is certain that the flat prohibition of eating any part of the pig was a real safeguard to the health of a nomad people who were accustomed to very little meat at any time, and who seldom had the facilities for thorough cooking.

The oldest of the Jewish fasts, that of the Day of Atonement, clearly was designed to serve as a symbolic reminder of the seriousness of human sin. In early Israelite usage individuals and communities established their own seasons of fasting *ad hoc,* as tokens of sorrow or of personal consecration. A number of standard fasts were added after the Babylonian Exile, most of them associated with critical events in the history of the Jewish people. Christian usage followed a similar principle, applying it first to Good Friday as a commemoration of our Lord's death, then to all Fridays and to the forty-day period of Lent, this last being understood as the Christian's sharing in Jesus' long struggle with temptation in the wilderness.

Here, just as in the case of the Sabbath, literalism could not but supervene. The motive often was lost in the mechanism, and so the mechanism more and more freely was wrested to accord with personal convenience. Every Jew has a collection of jokes about ways of dodging the dietary laws, as every Roman Catholic and Episcopalian has about devices used to circumvent the Lenten austerities. One English classic, of a slightly different kind, is the argument of the High Church Bishop Lancelot Andrewes. Andrewes seems genuinely to have believed in the observance of Lent on principle; but in concession to popular distaste for everything regarded as 'popish' he urged rather that the eating of fish on Friday was essential to preserve the British fishing industry, and so the British command of the narrow seas.

The Bishop failed wholly to impress the Puritans, and made little impact on the mass of the clergy and parishioners of the Church of England. Yet Puritanism, sternly rejecting the Catholic rule in its specifics, promptly created its own reasonably exact facsimile in other kinds of abstinence. Born in conflict and living in tension, the Reformed and Separatist groups in England found their life serious indeed. Accordingly, and because the Cavaliers were rather notably unserious, the English nonconformists made the basic test that of 'frivolity.' Accompanying this, and reflecting the economic concerns of the rising middle class from whose ranks the sects were recruited, was a strong disposition to equate improper conduct with what was expensive in money terms.

Thus, despite the dramatic stresses of *The Scarlet Letter,* typical American Puritan standards of behavior have been appreciably less concerned with sexual conduct, as such, than with such costly (and non-private) diversions as drinking, smoking, and the theatre. The recently discovered and much publicized practice of 'bundling,' a delight to the irreverent because it is supposed to scandalize the conventional, was a perfectly normal product of the New England climate in combination with the basic Puritan attitudes. Only last summer, myself a conventional person placed temporarily in an agrarian and dominantly Puritan setting, I said to a group of youngsters at a summer conference, 'I know some of you are shocked by my thinking that liquor and tobacco don't constitute fundamental religious issues. All I can say about that is that you're not half so shocked as I am by the way all of you act every night around this place as soon as it gets dark.'

It is of course true that there are serious moral aspects of the liquor question. Drinking constituted a major problem in British society in the eighteenth century, and had for centuries, largely because the island climate provided more readily for the production of potent spirits than for that of the more gentle wines. The corruption of the new eighteenth-century working class by over-indulgence in liquor unquestionably was what led to Mr. Wesley's intransigent attacks upon the traffic, and so to Methodist leadership in prohibitionist campaigns in more recent times. The common ban on smoking, however, scarcely is to be assigned to so serious and valid a cause; and its almost total absence from the culture of Protestantism in the American South suggests that here, as with the greater issue of slavery, the North found it easy to forbid what for it had proved unprofitable.

Mormonism presents an extremely interesting case, and one that is fully comprehensible in the light of its Puritan cultural ancestry. Bred in the rural Protestantism of upstate New York in the early nineteenth century, Joseph Smith not only maintained the prevailing taboos on liquor and tobacco, but in the 'Word of Wisdom' added to them even a fiat against the drinking of coffee. (Mormons have their own assortment of stories about manoeuvres designed to get around that one!) At the same time, and quite without any such 'immoral' intent as the fanatical enemies of Mormonism alleged, Smith asserted a positive religious value in sexual fulfillment. Polygyny is now outlawed within Mormonism as it is by the external command of the state; but the early recognition of a healthy freedom between the sexes is illustrated still in the fact that, of the typical Puritan restrictions, the one against social dancing is among Mormons conspicuous by its absence. Positively, indeed, the Church of Jesus Christ of the Latter Day Saints seems to have done a better job of providing wholesome recreation under religious auspices than has almost any other religious community.

The temporary and almost accidental nature of many quasi-religious taboos is exemplified by a curious phenomenon in the long existing legislation of the Methodist Episcopal Church, somewhat modified and quite significantly expanded at the time of the union with the Southern and Methodist Protestant Churches. In the former but not very distant days a candidate for admission to an Annual Conference as a 'Preacher on Trial' was required to answer in writing two questions, and two only:

(1) Are you in debt so as to embarrass you in the work of the Ministry? Answer: No.
(2) Will you wholly abstain from the use of tobacco? Answer: Yes.

The selection of these two items obviously reflects not a sober, long-term judgment as to what mattered most in the conduct of the clergy, but rather the spot action of General Conferences at times when (1) debt, and (2) tobacco, had become matters of special concern and discussion. It must be more or less circumstantial that sex and liquor, certainly more critical areas of behavior, were not dignified by this sort of special mention. Perhaps the reason is the encouraging one that more of the Methodist ministers smoked than drank, and that more of them failed to pay their bills than practised what in the strictly limited sense is called 'immorality.'

The present legislation of the Methodist Church, far more broadly conceived, requires

. . . written answers to questions which may be asked concerning such matters as his age, health, religious and church experience, call to the ministry, educational record, and plans.

Then it specifies that 'The following questions shall be included.' Among five listed are the two historic ones, but so decisively rephrased as wholly to change the emphasis:

(3) Are you in debt so as to interfere with your work, or have you obligations to others which will make it difficult for you to live on the salary you are to receive?

(4) Will you abstain from the use of tobacco and other indulgences which may injure your influence?

My informants from Conferences in the American South tell me, however, that despite the mandatory 'shall' the fourth question usually is not asked on the sunny side of the Mason-Dixon line.

What the Methodists have done in their rewriting marks a return to consideration of motive, and so to concern for others as a primary factor in making rules for one's self. This is where Jesus and St. Paul stood, and where the Church at its best and most thoughtful ever has placed the emphasis. 'The sabbath was made for man,' said Jesus, 'not man for the sabbath.' I remember that when as a small boy I read that, I knew it couldn't mean what it seemed to say: for certainly my grandfather regarded man, and juveniles in particular, as having been made for the express purpose of observing (on Sunday) a Sabbath of infinite privation and correspondingly infinite duration. Most of historic Christianity has understood Jesus better than my grandfather did; and Sunday rightly is what continental Europe always has considered it to be, a day of worship first and withal one of full personal freedom from the strains of the working week.

St. Paul had to tread a narrow and tricky path between Jewish rigidities on the one hand and pagan license on the other. His advice on that point, as is typical with him, is eminently practical. Twice in the letter we know as I Corinthians he says, 'All things are lawful for me, but all things are not expedient.' The Christians who are troubled about meat that has been offered to pagan idols are counseled:

Whatsoever is sold in the shambles, that eat, asking no question for conscience sake. For the earth is the Lord's, and the fullness thereof. If any of them that believe not bid you to a feast, and ye be disposed to go; whatsoever is set before you, eat, asking no questions for conscience sake. But if any man say unto you, This is offered in sacrifice unto idols, eat it not for his sake that showed it, and for conscience sake: for the earth is the Lord's, and the fullness thereof: Conscience, I say, not thine own, but of the other . . .

The apostle's own position and practice are summed up, in the same letter, in the classic, 'If meat make my brother to offend, I will eat no flesh while the world standeth.'

Since we have noted an illustration from current Methodism, we ought also to remember what John Wesley had to say on this issue. Writing from Georgia in 1737 to a certain Mrs. Chapman, Wesley protested:

> You seem to apprehend that I believe religion to be inconsistent with cheerfulness, and with a sociable, friendly temper. So far from it, that I am convinced, as true religion or holiness cannot be without cheerfulness, so steady cheerfulness, on the other hand, cannot be without holiness or true religion. And I am equally convinced that true religion has nothing sour, austere, unsociable, unfriendly, in it; but, on the contrary, implies the most winning sweetness, the most amiable softness and gentleness.

With reference to fasting and other self-imposed disciplines, Wesley went on to say:

> Do you refuse no pleasure but what is a hindrance to some greater good, or has a tendency to some evil? It is my very rule; and I know no other by which a sincere, reasonable Christian can be guided. In particular, I pursue this rule in eating, which I seldom do without much pleasure.

It should be a comfort to many to know that Wesley, who fasted consistently every Wednesday and Friday of the year, and urged his followers to do likewise, nevertheless enjoyed his food the rest of the time. What is much more important, however, is that Wesley enjoyed his life. It was not an easy life that he lived. It was a life full of self-discipline, as in the seeking of the 'greater good' he conformed to stringent monastic rules of fasting and devotion that he laid down for himself. It was a life full of struggle, as the Church of the time assailed him because he insisted on taking his Christianity so seriously. Nevertheless Wesley liked to eat, and nevertheless he persisted in steady cheerfulness.

Clear understanding of these principles as followed by Jesus, St. Paul, and Wesley should at once cure Christians of taking out their religious enthusiasm in negativity, and non-Christians of supposing that there is anything inherently negative in the Christian motive. Where negatives appear, they are made so by the positive importance of the greater good. In any such surrender of the trivial, for the sake of the essential, there is room for no self-pity, for no vestige of lugubriousness. 'When ye fast,' said Jesus, 'be not . . . of a sad countenance.' The Christian who fasts for the sake of the kingdom has in his fasting nothing to be sad about.

The details of fasting, and of its equivalents, necessarily will vary from culture to culture and from time to time. Cultural lag commonly preserves both taboo and license past the periods of their true social usefulness. Both license and taboo, therefore, need frequently to be reconsidered in terms of their relevance in each new day. It is the principle that remains unchanged, the principle of relative value. On that principle, and on the resultant pattern of a defensible hierarchy of values, churchmen and the unchurched are likely to agree much more than they will differ. All that is necessary for mutual understanding is that each of them, facing a historic sumptuary negative, or a new one, shall ask sincerely the simple question, 'Why?'

It is time to turn to the affirmative side. Here the notion that religious people can't have fun is as meaningless as the still enduring American superstition that no Englishman has a sense of humor. Mostly, it just isn't so. Marginally, it is a matter of how 'fun' and 'humor' are to be identified. We have seen that the Christian has a considered rationale for setting certain limits to his behavior: some of them direct, such as refraining from drinking to the point of drunkenness, and some of them symbolic, such as periodical fasting and abstinence. The limits, however, are to be imposed for reasons. Where there is no reason against pleasure, then pleasure is authentically a fulfillment of the wholeness of the Christian life.

Jesus himself was accused of being 'a gluttonous man and a winebibber,' and of running with the wrong crowd. Nor did he seem to resent this, nor offer any denial. Instead, he merely pointed out that in his time, as today, there simply is no pleasing those who stay apart to scoff. They objected alike to John's fasting and to Jesus' eating and drinking, to John's solitude and to Jesus' sociability; and so they sound uncommonly like a good many of the bystanders of our own time. The facts in the two cases are evident. John had no time for fun. Jesus had only a little, but that he used with full enthusiasm.

A striking example of the balance which the Church has sought stands in the establishment of the Fourth Sunday in Lent as one of rejoicing and even of gaiety. Called *Laetare* in Catholicism, 'Refreshment Sunday' in English usage, this day is marked by the substitution of rose-colored frontal and antependia for the dark Lenten violet, by the return of flowers to the altar, and by the singing of joyous music otherwise avoided in the Lenten season. A similar usage marks *Gaudete*, the Third Sunday in Advent. In both cases a time of solemn self-examination is deliberately interrupted by the reminder that God is a God of joy as well as of stern command, that man in Christ is called on to be·glad as well as to be sober.

They who are the surest of their religious foundation are the most readily able to be gay about it. The Catholics and Jews, taking their faith for granted and never doubting its ultimate validity, delight to tell stories about the foibles both of their clergy and of their laymen. Some other groups, *per contra*, by their very sensitivity to ridicule announce their deep-rooted doubts of their own position. He who has confidence in himself can afford to laugh at himself. He who has confidence in his religious values equally can afford to be gay about them, because he is fundamentally happy within them.

When it comes to sheer gaiety, springing from a fully joyous heart and tinged by no bitterness, the religious person has a striking advantage over the irreligious. Compare, for example, the ebullience and lightheartedness of a Methodist Conference, without benefit of highballs, with the forced witticisms heard at a Saturday night binge of the leftist intelligentsia. (I speak with knowledge: I have frequented both.) Who has real fun? He who has joy in his heart; and that is he who has religion there. 'The earth is the Lord's, and the fullness thereof.' 'This is the day [any day] which the Lord hath made; we will rejoice and be glad in it.'

It was a very strong temptation to make this chapter a mosaic *au* Bennett Cerf. Hitherto I have resisted; and now I am glad, for during this writing I have concluded that some time I must compile my own ecclesiastical joke book. But I must end now with the favorite of all my favorites. It belongs here not only because it is funny, not only because it illustrates fun within a religious setting, but also because its evident moral is one that both the religious and the irreligious ought to heed. Of its veracity (if anyone cares) there can be no doubt, for it was told to me by an Episcopal rector in Massachusetts.

It appears that this gentleman was one of a party of tourists who were being shown around one of the old English cathedrals. Their guide was the verger: one of those grand old men who apparently had been born just about the time that the building's foundations were laid, and who had been growing up with it ever since. Proudly the old gentleman led the visitors through the structure. He dated its every wall and transept and bay and spire, and wellnigh every pane of glass in the great windows. He recited the heroic deeds of the knights of old, whose effigies lay graven in stone upon their tombs. He pointed to the battle flags hanging dusty and tattered from the arches, and spoke of the wars of long ago.

At last he brought the party up to the chancel railing. Now this was one of those old-fashioned railings, with the entry marked on either side by a large, round, wooden knob. Before one of these knobs the verger paused, and portentously cleared his throat. 'Now, ladies and gentlemen,' he said, 'I wants you to notice this here post. This here post, ladies and gentlemen, is most important. This here post, ladies and gentlemen, already has been confirmed by two nearsighted Bishops.'

The Bishops then, being nearsighted, had wasted divine unction on dead lumber. So also has the Church, whenever it has made its negations an end in themselves instead of a means toward the greater good. But equally has nearsightedness afflicted those who from outside have shared in the error of confusing lifeless wood with living human value, and who therefore have concluded that the Church contains nothing but lumberheads. Let them correct their vision, as of course the Bishops and all we churchmen should too. Let all of us know that God has made us to laugh when things are funny. Then, instead of frowning both ways, we can rejoice in fun and games together.

CONCLUSION

*on the religiousness
of the irreligious*

⏏ The word which St. Paul in his speech on Mars Hill used to describe his Athenian audience, in the Greek *deisidaimon*, literally 'fearing the deity(ies),' is an ambiguous one. In general earlier Greek authors used it in a favorable sense, later ones unfavorably. Chronologically, and perhaps in meaning as well, Paul stands in the middle.

Recent translators of the New Testament have chosen to present the former emphasis, by reading 'very religious' rather than 'too superstitious.' That 'religious' is what Paul really meant seems likely, for the whole beginning of his speech is a complimentary and ingratiating one. He does not condemn the men of Athens for having erected their altar To THE UNKNOWN GOD. He argues only that the time has come when they may know him.

In one way our modern Athenians, *deisidaimonesteroi*, are less to be excused than were the ancient ones. In the middle of the first century the Christian message was young indeed, and up to Paul's arrival none in Athens had had a chance to hear it. In the middle of the twentieth century Christianity stands as a major molder of our culture, and lives all about them who prefer to keep their God still unknown.

I have called these modern unbelievers superstitious because they have chosen to fear and to avoid without ever having used their abundant opportunity to learn and to know; and that mood is the very essence of superstition. Yet the real tragedy of the whole case is that in truth the great majority of the self-consciously irreligious are not irreligious at all. They are devout seekers of truth, so long as it is not called 'religion.' They are loyal defenders of value, most of whose sources they have forgotten or ignore. They use and love their own symbols, a bit naïvely perhaps but very sincerely. They honestly seek the well being of man, and they work earnestly toward the making of a better world. In short, they are religious men and women.

How sad it is, then, that in this one realm of religious awareness, superstition has them so firmly in its grip. How much better they would understand themselves if they knew whence their dearest values came. How much better adjusted they would be in the world if they could but recognize their essential membership in a world force they have affected to despise. Common fairness requires that they should examine the data. (I do not say 'reëxamine,' for they have not examined yet.) Their own intelligence, working on the data, will do the rest.

If after investigation they decide against religion, that is their privilege. At least then they will be entitled to an opinion, which now they are not. He who rejects for reasons even then may be mistaken, but he is intellectually respectable and to be respected. It is just the rejecting of religion without reasons that is the mark of irreligious superstition.

'I decided long ago to get along without religion,' a distinguished friend of mine told me. 'So anything you like,' I challenged, 'is by definition not religious.' He nodded assent. This is no way to define religion; and to identify religion in terms of its least authentic and least meaningful expressions is not the way either. This gentleman, and most of those of whom I have been speaking, discount religion because they suppose it uninformed and irrational. I repeat again the charge: that they themselves are uninformed and irrational, and therefore utterly superstitious, until they seek authentic information on the subject, and until they do some sober reasoning about it.

If any of them have stayed with me this far, they are permitted to read on to the end. But I do not deceive myself as to where the majority of readers of this enquiry will be found. The superstitious, wedded to their superstition, mostly will not step outside the bonds of their miscegenation. Rather the religious, like these others quite human in preferring to read what already they believe, will provide the bulk of the audience. There therefore have to be two conclusions: and this second one addressed to us who are in the Church, who count ourselves religious people.

Who is most to blame for current irreligion, for current contempt of religious faith and religious institutions? Who but we? We are the bearers of the tradition we accept and love. We are its representatives in the world. We are those, then, by whose measure the world will judge the faith that we profess. If there has been failure, it is we who have failed.

The 'too superstitious' are in truth very religious. If they are to escape the bonds of the superstition that has held them up to now, if they are to grow into full consciousness of the religion that is implicit within them, that revival of understanding will have to begin in us. Not until our own religion is worthy can we present its case effectively to others. Unless it is worthy, we have no case to present.

This means that we shall have to be all we claim to be as religious persons. We must know such real joy in our allegiance that our gladness will be evident and enviable. We must make the fellowship of our faith so real, so mighty, that the world no longer can think to ignore or discount this living body of the Christ. To that end we are challenged to live our ideals absolutely, knowing the cost and willing without reservation to pay it.

In the world of human relationships we are called to make our noblest values effective in every dealing of man with man, and of nation with nation. We may not retreat into a tower here, nor think to substitute a heaven hereafter. In our use of symbols, which we shall continue because we know our symbols meaningful for us, we shall hold clearly the distinction between occasional form and ultimate reality.

As students we are required to learn all the facts, and to dodge none of their implications. In our thinking then we shall be clearheaded and fearless, assured that only the truth will make us free. We need to be better acquainted with the details of our tradition than now we are, in order both to appreciate it fully and to represent it worthily. All of this means that we shall continue to learn and to grow, in the vitality that ever has marked the heritage of which rightly we are so proud.

'When the Son of man cometh, shall he find faith on the earth?' The faith has endured because those who were before us have sought earnestly, thought bravely, chosen decisively, lived in absolute fidelity. The contagion of that faith has caught us, to our own great happiness. It is ours, if we meet the conditions, to pass the contagion on. Only if we do meet the conditions will our 'too superstitious' join us where they belong, in the company of the truly religious.